30-Minute Meals with God

Endorsement

Lynn Williams' "Devotional Cookbook for Godly Living" is the most comprehensive and compelling book on spiritual food that I have read. Lynn's professional background and Christian walk are evident as she introduces the reader to the intricacies of culinary art to illuminate God's desire that we realize spiritual maturity. From childhood we learn that daily intake of nutritious food is necessary for healthy biological, cognitive, and emotional development. Nutritional loss compromises overall health and wellness, and may lead to death. Equally important to healthy living is spiritual development. Lynn guides the reader through spiritual food groups, menus, and utensils required to develop a personal relationship with the Lord in order to attain spiritual maturity. All aspects of food preparation are examined, such as "food safety" and "soul contamination." Actual recipes from an appetizer to a dessert add to the uniqueness of this book. Matthew 5:6 states, "You're blessed when you've worked up a good appetite for God. He's food and drink; the best meal you'll ever eat."

Read and be blessed!
—**M. Jean Peacock, PhD**

The Royal Candlelight

30-Minute Meals with God:
The Devotional Cookbook
for
Godly Living

by Lynn Williams
Your Spiritual Gourmet Chef

Royal Candlelight Christian Publishing Company
"Royalty in the Making"

The Royal Candlelight: 30-Minute Meals with God
© 2010 by Lynn Williams

Royal Candlelight Christian Publishing Company
"Royalty in the Making"

Royal Candlelight Christian Publishing
P.O. Box 3021
Fontana, California 92334
www.royalcandlelight.com
info@royalcandlelight.com
Internet TV Website: Ustream tv.com (Royal Candlelight)

Editor: Rachel Starr Thomson
Graphic & Media Arts Designer: Talon Williams
Book Layout Designer: Nicole Dunlap
Sales & Marketing Director: Paul Williams
Website Designer: Ebenezer Jesutimi

ISBN-10: 0615822290
ISBN-13: 978-0615822297

Printed in the United States of America

Dedications

To my husband, Paul, who is my greatest inspiration,
my children and grandchildren,
and all my brothers and sisters in Christ, who are concerned about
their spiritual growth
and have a desire to draw closer in their relationship with God.

Special Appreciation

Alice Smith
Shirley Simmons
Cynthia Williams

Table of Contents

Your Spiritual Gourmet Chef's Seven Personal Food Recipes
Your Spiritual Gourmet Chef has prepared some personal recipes for you so that you can experience *a mountain of joy* that will give you a little taste of *heaven* as you become *trustworthy* in studying and seeking God through this devotional cookbook. These recipes, both physical and spiritual, will become *delightfully delicious* to you as you get *Spirit-filled* on the Word of God and become *fruitful and take dominion* over your life by taking time to *stay devoted and be blessed* by the Master Chef.

SPIRITUAL A LA CARTE

Drink Recipe
Mt. Caramel Chocolate Shake
A Mountain of Joy
Page 28

Appetizer Recipe
Angel Shrimp & Crab Stuffed Eggs
Heavenly
Page 81

Soup Recipe
Faithful Seafood Soup
Trustworthy
Page 95

Salad Recipe
Joyful Broccoli & Raisin Salad
Delightfully Delicious
Page 103

Giving Thanks for the Food

"How sweet are Your words to my taste,
sweeter than honey to my mouth."
—Psalm 119:103

I would like to give honor and thanks by expressing my deepest gratitude to God my heavenly Father; Jesus Christ, my Lord and Savior; and the Holy Spirit, my Teacher and Guide. Thank You,

Lord, for giving me Your Word so that I might taste and see for myself that You are good as the Word shows me that You are the Lord my God. The Bible has become the most precious book in my possession. It makes me feel just like Jeremiah did when he said, "And Thy words became for me a joy and the delight of my heart: for I have been called by Thy name" (Jeremiah 15:16, KJV) So thank You, Lord, for choosing and calling this servant vessel to serve up one of the greatest meals any human being can feast on!

To my pastor, Dr. Joshua Beckley, and my Ecclesia Christian Fellowship holy family: with you, I continue to grow spiritually, which has allowed me to use my spiritual gifts freely, and this in turn has given me plenty of opportunity to learn how to love and care for God's people by assisting in picking up the broken pieces of their lives.

My Prayer Recipe

Dear Lord,

Incline my heart to Thyself, O Lord,
so that I may walk in all Your ways
in order to keep Your commandments, Your statutes,
and Your ordinances which You command.
Let my heart therefore be wholly devoted to You, Lord,
so that the world may know that You, Lord, are God
and there is no one else like You or above You.
I desire to walk in integrity of heart and uprightness,
doing according to all that You have commanded;
to love You with all my heart, mind, soul, and strength;
and to serve and worship no other gods.
As for me and my house, we will only serve
You, O Lord, forever.
Amen.

Foreword

*a*s a pastor, you work hard to help people grow and understand that how their relationship with Christ is more than just a part of their lives. The gospel will not only give them peace of mind, but will literally transform and change the very conduct and condition of their lives. The Word of God not only gives life, it *is* life.

It is a great joy and a great satisfaction to come across a saint, a believer, a church member who not only believes this, but applies it. I'm so excited for Lynn Williams and the work she has done with this daily devotional guide. It is a great tool for those who seek to grow and deepen their relationship with Christ. The thoughtfulness and detail with which she explains and makes application of the tools and the Word of God demonstrates that she is one who has experienced what she has written.

What I like most about this devotional guide is that it takes a new and different approach to the study of the Word from an analogy that we commonly use: food! The Word is referred to as the "Bread of Life" in John 6:33 and 35, "meat" in Hebrews 5:12 (KJV), and "milk" in 1 Peter 2:2. Lynn's analogies come from her experience and knowledge as a professional chef and caterer.

The terms *master chef* and *sous chef* take on all new meaning in this study guide, along with other terms, like *fruit drink, appetizers, salads, entrées, desserts,* and *sweet treats.* Lynn has prepared a spiritual meal that the spiritual palate cannot resist! You will dine sumptuously on the delicacies prepared for you under the leading of the Holy Spirit in her life.

I am truly excited about the blessing you are about to receive as you discipline yourself through this devotional guide. The feast you are about to partake of is fit for a King's kid, and your Father has chosen one of His Master Sous Chefs to prepare it for you. Truly, in this devotional guide, you will taste and see that the Lord is good!

God bless you, and dine well!

Pastor Joshua Beckley, PhD

Ecclesia Christian Fellowship, San Bernardino, California

Acknowledgments

Thanks go to my husband, Paul, who has been my greatest comfort and support for the last thirty-two years. He has continued to be my inspiration and has shown me by example how to love others. It is by watching him as he places others before himself that I have grown to understand and see how God blesses those who follow this command. My husband granted me the freedom to spend as much time as was necessary in the writing of this book with my heavenly Father without ever complaining, which allowed me to accomplish this task set before me.

I thank God for my parents, Charles and Doris Patterson, who provided me at a very young age with a strong Christian foundation. I have tried to pass it on and instill it in my three special gifts from God, my children. I'm so grateful that my parents are still alive and well today, and that they continue to invest in all our lives.

Thanks to my wonderful children, Kimberly, Walter, and Talon, who have all been blessings from God—not to forget my two beautiful grandchildren, Jeremy and Briana, who are truly God's offspring. They are learning, at the very young ages of ten and seven, how to love and give to God as they love and share with one another as well as with others. My prayer is that all my children and grandchildren will grow to be strong men and women of God, filled with the Holy Spirit, devoted and mature in Christ Jesus.

A special thanks to all of my family members: the Patterson family, the Smith family, and the Williams family. Our families are truly blessed by God because of the strong spiritual foundation which has been passed down from generation to generation.

Several individuals have played significant roles in my life, helping me come into the knowledge of who God is and what is the purpose for my life. My pastor, Joshua Beckley, has been a great influence because of his outstanding integrity, his knowledge and understanding of God's Word, and his dedication to the people of God. He is truly a man of

God, with the ability to lead God's people to do great things for the edification of the body of Christ and His kingdom. My brother in Christ, Minister Robert Strong, has been a great influence as my spiritual brother and executive director, encouraging me and helping in my spiritual development by giving me the opportunity to express and communicate the Word of God in various ways. My Ecclesia Church family deserves to be thanked for the love they share one for another and for the great fellowship we experience each time we are together. I appreciate those church members who have allowed me the opportunity to grow in my spiritual gifts, especially teaching. Your enthusiasm has encouraged me to continue to study to show myself approved unto God, which has made me realize what an awesome responsibility it is to share the gospel.

To my beloved ministry team members, whom I have come to know and love so dearly, I say thank you for your dedication to the callings upon your lives and services. Your joy and commitment are one of the reasons I find great joy in serving God's people.

To the Christian who wishes to know God personally and become approved by God by studying His Word: I hope you will find this spiritual "cookbook" useful and helpful in meeting your spiritual needs as you become a conscious, healthy eater of the Word of God.

To the unbeliever who doesn't know God personally: I hope you will find this devotional cookbook for godly living your key to opening the door and let the truth of who God is into your heart, so He can come in and allow the Master Chef to serve you His wonderful "Soup for Salvation" to eternal life.

Introduction

Your Spiritual Gourmet Chef's Personal Kitchen

Bonjour, sweet Prince and Princess!

Several years ago as I was getting ready to go to church, I was watching a televised service when the minister made what I felt was a very terrible statement. Trying to illustrate the closeness of Jesus, he referred to Jesus as "my dog"—using a slang term for the closeness of friends. That statement felt like someone had just stabbed me in the heart. Words are profound, and they have set meanings. I don't recall anywhere in God's Word where dogs are referenced in a positive way. My spirit grieved because God's name is holy and should never be used in such a manner.

As I started to change the channel, I heard the Holy Spirit speak to me and say, "Now watch the response of those who call themselves my children." The congregation's response was even more shocking and upsetting, because they responded as if this minister had spoken profoundly. They were jumping and shouting as if they had just won a million dollars.

At the very sight of this, I began to cry. Why did God's people not know that this statement was one of blasphemy? Instead of lifting the Savior up, this preacher brought the Savior down to where He was equal to us—and even lower than we are. Then I heard a still, small voice that whispered to my heart, *"My people perish for lack of knowledge."*

For over a year, this was the message I continued to hear from God. Finally, after a year had gone by, I asked God, "Since these are Your people, Lord, what can I do about their lack of knowledge?" Right then, I remembered an old song that says that God uses ordinary people. At that moment, I realized that I was just an ordinary person with a love for God and a love for my sisters and brothers in Christ. Those who are willing to be used by God are called, prepared, trained and equipped by Him to do the work He has called them to do. They become His mouth, His hands, and His feet to speak, do, and go wherever necessary to express the love He has for mankind.

Finally, I sat down one day at the dinner table to talk with God. You see, I am a Certified Gourmet Chef with a degree in French cooking. I have a desire to own my own restaurant to serve people, especially my brothers and sisters in Christ who, I believe, deserve to be treated like royalty (we are all the King's children, are we not?). I also wanted to (someday) write a recipe book. And I wanted to talk to God about all of this while at the dinner table.

However, while at the table I decided to put God first by laying my personal desires aside. I asked Him, "Lord, what would *You* have me do for You that would be pleasing to You and give You glory?" I was truly willing to give up my dreams and desires and focus on the One whom I have crowned King of my life, since He knows what is best for His little princess. I believed that maybe God had something else planned for my life, and for me to concentrate on my own desires was hindering me from doing His will based on those plans.

To my surprise, in my willingness to please God, I found my own desires right in the middle of His will for my life—but from a different perspective. The result is this recipe book.

I have found great joy in pleasing God. God says in His Word that if we delight in Him, He will give us the desires of our hearts (Psalm 37:4). Often, we as Christians struggle to take that step of faith. It is not because we have doubts about God's ability to do the impossible, but because we question whether or not God will work things out like we think they ought to be worked out. Sometimes, we don't like God's decisions even though they are for our good. We tend to base decisions on our emotions and on what we can see at that time, so it's hard sometimes to see what is good for us. However, when we look back, we will see that God knew exactly what He was doing, and His works always turn out for our good and His glory. You see, everything comes from God, everything happens through God, and everything ends up for God (Romans 11:36: "For of Him and through Him and to Him are all things, to whom be the glory forever. Amen").

My prayer is that this "recipe book for godly living" will lead you into an exciting appreciation for God's Word and ultimate dependency on Him to guide you through your lifelong Christian journey. I pray that you will taste all the wonderful flavors of His Word and experience the textures of His love for you. I pray that God will fill you up with the truth of Christ, which will not only draw you closer in your relationship with Him, but give you the knowledge and confidence needed to share your spiritual dining experiences with others and bring the glory and honor that are due to the name of Jesus.

Throughout this book, my focus will be on teaching you a method of studying God's Word for yourself. Interestingly, my confirmation in this focus came from my daughter, who loves the Lord dearly and has been in church her entire thirty-eight years. One day, she called me to discuss the difficult decision of changing churches. I was saddened to hear that even though she has a great desire to know God, attends church regularly, and works faithfully in ministry, she realized that she really did not know how to study the Bible. After her consultation with God, she made the decision to go where she felt she would gain more wisdom and knowledge in the Word of God from a strong, Bible-teaching church. She wanted to be under a church that has a heart for God and where the Bible is being explained, taught, demonstrated, and applied through biblical instructions by those whose motives are for God's children to spiritually grow and mature in the Word as they develop their relationships with Christ—as described in Jeremiah 3:15: "Then I will give you shepherds after My own heart, who will feed you on knowledge and understanding" (NASB). You see, instead of praying and allowing the Holy Spirit to direct and guide your decision;

many Christians change churches for various reasons based on their own personal decisions. They become disappointed or upset with their personal experience at their church. They may want to go to a church closer to home or they want to see if they can get a position of leadership to promote their own personal agenda. They may also look to see if the church has a place for their children to go to help in their decision. All these reasons as well as others may be important to you, but your number one goal for changing churches should be about your spiritual growth and if the church is teaching the Word of God so you can rightly divide the word of truth.

It wasn't long before my daughter became tremendously excited, because she had learned more in one year there than in all of her years just listening to messages without knowing how to study the Word for herself! For the first time, at that moment I realized that attending church regularly and even working diligently in ministry will not necessarily increase our knowledge of who God is if we are not following God's instruction to study His Word for ourselves (2 Timothy 2:15).

In these pages, I've attempted to open to you the banquet room of God's Word. Of course, since I am a gourmet chef, I'll be doing so with culinary style and artistry.

Therefore, my brothers and sisters sit back and enjoy this wonderful adventure while I take you on a spiritual journey through a spiritual world filled with culinary pleasures to help you explore and discover the wonderful Spirit-filled flavors of God's meals. They have been prepared just for you to dine on.

Chapter 1

Come and Dine
A Spiritual Objective

"Be diligent to present yourself approved to God, a worker who does not need to be ashamed, rightly dividing the word of truth."
—2 Timothy 2

Chapter 1
Come and Dine: A Spiritual Objective

The goal of dining on the Word of God is to become spiritually strong and healthy. Daily time at the "dinner table" of the Word is an opportunity to develop an intimate relationship with God as you get into the habit of spending time with Him, eating home-cooked meals that have been slowly cooked over thousands of years to intensify every blend of intense and powerful flavors—spices of love and special, sweet herbs of compassion. (Our God doesn't microwave!) The Master Chef, Jesus Christ, has invested time and effort into cooking for us. It is beneficial to our spirits to spend these precious minutes with the King on a regular basis, partaking of His Word and investing in our eternal futures, just as we regularly build up our bodies by eating physical food.

Every human being is made up of spirit, soul, and body (1 Thessalonians 5:23). Society has taught us to focus on our physical bodies without really giving any thought to our spirits—to the part of us that we'll call, for the sake of analogy, our *spiritual body*. The spiritual body is just as important as the physical one, and yet, as Christians, we often neglect it. How foolish we can be! If anything, our spiritual bodies require *more* attention than our physical bodies. It is the part of us that will live for eternity.

We know that our physical bodies cannot go a long time without eating and drinking. We also know that if we eat and drink the wrong things, our bodies will become weak and sickly. Eventually, we can destroy our bodies, contributing to our own death because of bad eating habits. The same thing is true of our spiritual body. If we don't feed our spirits regularly, they will also become weak and sickly. We need the Word of God within us to control and fight off spiritual sickness and diseases from Satan, worldly desires, and our own sinful flesh.

Anything that requires food, if not fed, will die. If we do not practice spiritually eating what is good for us by *studying the Word of God,* then we will cause our own spiritual death—a tragic separation from God who is our strength and the supplier of all our physical and spiritual needs.

No meal is richer than those offered up in the Word of God for His children to CHEW *(Christians Having Eternal Wealth)* on. Our spiritual objective is not only to build you up in spiritual health, but to make you aware of the fine ingredients of the Word so that you may appreciate them and glorify God as you eat.

Two ingredients are especially important: In each recipe for life in the Bible, *Lamb*, the richest part of any meal, is the Main Secret Ingredient. To find out who Jesus is, look for the Lamb of God, His words, and His works in every book of the Bible. Take notes, because you won't know who you are in Christ until you know who He is in you.

The second most important ingredient in the Bible is *the child of God.* Since the Bible was written for God's children, you can also know who *you* should be in Christ by examining every character mentioned in the Bible. Learn the responsibilities, blessings, and promises made to you, as well as the conditions, commands, warnings, errors, and consequences that apply to you. As the Word feeds your spirit, you will be made pleasing to our Lord and Savior, Jesus Christ.

To be a child of God is the most glorious and exalted privilege we could ever have, and the privilege of dining on God's meals is free. We should, however, consider the cost of the food and what it took to freely offer it to us—after all, it was the Master Chef's responsibility to determine if the price He paid was too high. He spared no cost in giving His life that we might have the best quality meals to last us for an eternity.

Chapter 2

The Master Chef

"He is the Rock, His work is perfect; for all His ways are justice,
a God of truth and without injustice; righteous and upright is He."
—*Deuteronomy 32:4*

Chapter 2
The Master Chef

*T*he title of *Master Chef* is often abused and misunderstood. The word *chef* in French means *chief* or *head*. Many leaders claim the title. But "Master Chef" should be reserved for Jesus Christ alone: He is the only divine Chief and Head of everything! He is the Master in charge of this universal kitchen (Colossians 1:18).

Jesus's title has been earned by experience, not only in the preparation of food, but also in managing His spiritual culinary staff and planning food production on a divinely skillful level. He has a thorough knowledge of everything. He understands organization and how to motivate people. He has a great understanding of planning menus, budgeting and controlling costs, purchasing food supplies, production procedures, food safety, and all the equipment used in His universal kitchen.

In examining the skills and attributes of the Master Chef, we find that cooking is a dynamic, professional art that provides great challenges as well as great rewards. As we come to the dining table of the Word, we will find that in every verse, chapter, and passage, there is always a level of perfection attained. The Master Chef has used His ability to seek out and purchase the best possible ingredients. In every meal, His expertise is shown through His great wisdom, power, knowledge, and understanding. Good cooking is the result of carefully developing the best possible flavors and perfect textures in every dish. As you feast on the Word of God, you will find that every teaching, every story, and every admonition is perfect.

The Word of God may have involved many writers who assisted

in preparing God's meals, but the Master Chef is ultimately responsible for the management of every meal. Since microwave cooking has its drawbacks, the Master Chef decided to spend thousands of years preparing these meals. The Bible consistently shows unity as well as diversity because God was the Divine Author behind each book, although He used many human authors to compose them. We are not exactly told which was the earliest book written, but there are two possibilities: Genesis and Job. Some believe that Job was written before Genesis due to some of the events that took place in Job, which gives the impression that his story occurred before the Mosaic Law. The last book composed was Revelation, written in AD 90. God's Sous Chefs (apostles, prophets, evangelists, pastors, and teachers) assisted Him in slowly cooking the divine selection of meals to preserve the special flavors in each dish, which are still good and flavorful today. God used the right amount of heat to produce the right flavors, aromas, textures, colors, and nutritional contents. He has a great knowledge of how our bodies assimilate foods, giving Him the freedom to develop various dishes that will meet our spiritual needs as the King's children.

Jesus Christ has an amazing and fascinating history. Getting to know Him through His recipes—His teachings, parables, and stories—is the best way to appreciate His great choices, His responsibility for the meals we enjoy, and the opportunities that await us as we follow His prescriptions for godly living.

One of the most wonderful attributes of the Master Chef is His commitment to service. He has never lost sight of the importance of excellent service and of providing quality food that is safe and properly cooked, well seasoned, and attractively presented. His commandments of perfection are consistent with His character. He has never asked us to do anything that He would not do or has not done Himself. He is the perfect example of how we are to provide excellent service to one another.

Even though the Sous Chefs had a stake in getting things done correctly in His universal kitchen, the Master Chef shouldered the ultimate responsibility for the success of His recipes—the teachings of the Bible. Every word is crafted by His abilities and expertise.

As we prepare to feast, let us pause for a moment to raise our spiritual glasses, which hold the Aged Royal Wine (the Holy Spirit who abides in us) to give all gratitude to the Master Chef!

Chapter 3

The Culinary Artistry of the Sous Chefs

"And He Himself gave some to be apostles, some prophets, some evangelists, and some pastors and teachers."
—Ephesians 4:1

Chapter 3
The Culinary Artistry of the Sous Chefs

*T*he Master Chef's assistants, the Sous Chefs (pronounced "sue chefs") were completely under the divine control of God Himself as they worked to prepare the meals of Scripture. Many of their names are familiar to us: Moses, David, Isaiah, Ezra, Luke, Matthew, James, Paul. Each was personally selected by the Master Chef, Jesus Christ. They came from various parts of the world, and they brought expertise from different cultural backgrounds to present the greatest feast ever known to mankind. The skill levels required of them were based on the standards of a great establishment—God's kingdom. The position of Sous Chef was very demanding; however, these men exemplified remarkable skills and dedicated their lives to innovation and obedience to the Highest Order.

God designed and filled the position of each Sous Chef based on special qualifications needed for the preparation of the sixty-six meals in His recipe book, the Bible. The four levels of Sous Chefs designated to fulfill the Master Chef's goals of perfection were:

Apostles: These were the men the Master Chef appointed and dispatched as ambassadors or messengers of God. However, they could never be greater than the Master Chef, Jesus Christ, who sent them out. God chose them to be witnesses before the world and thus solidified their authority in the positions they held. Apostleship was a limited position—nowhere in the Bible are churches instructed to ordain apostles. This was a position assigned and filled strictly by God. (Acts 1:2, "Until the day when He was taken up after he had by the Holy Spirit given orders to the apostles whom He had chosen.")

Paul and Matthew were among the apostles.

Prophets: Prophets were the foretellers (not fortune-tellers) of future events. They were interpreters who spoke under the divine influence and inspiration of God, speaking not from their own thoughts, but from what they received from God—unlike fortune-tellers, who are under the influence of their master, Satan. (Acts 16:16 reads "And it happened that as we were going to the place of prayer, a certain slave-girl having a spirit of divination met us, who was bringing her masters much profit by fortunetelling. NASB) New Testament prophets were a class of instructors or preachers, next in rank to apostles and before teachers. God made known His divine secrets and mysteries through the prophets to generally reveal His purposes for His people. The New Testament prophets assisted the Christian church much as the Old Testament prophets assisted Israel: as an immediate connection between God, the Israelites, and the church. Such prophets were not ordained in local churches, nor did they have successors. The office of the prophets should not be confused with those who have the gift of prophecy. Remember that those who prophesy are not necessarily prophets in the Old or New Testament sense of this restricted position. Among the prophets who functioned as Sous Chefs in the Word of God are Moses, Isaiah, and Jeremiah.

Evangelists: Evangelists were preachers. Often, they were not assigned to any particular church or location, but traveled as missionaries to declare the good news by preaching the gospel and establishing churches. They were men of good testimony; filled with the Holy Spirit and wisdom from on high. The Word of God speaks highly of several evangelists and records some of their words, including Philip and Apollos.

Pastors and Teachers: These were shepherds who were responsible for pasturing and teaching as they cared for their flocks (Ephesians 4:12). They were the ones who watched over and provided for the welfare of the church as a whole and were considered spiritual guides of their churches in particular. James, the brother of Jesus, was a great teacher.

The Sous Chefs were able to test their cooking skills and culinary artistry against the standards of their Mentor, the Master Chef Jesus Christ. They successfully prepared and completed each meal in Scripture because they learned from the *best.*

Chapter 4

A Special Purchase and Measuring Cup

"In Him we have redemption through His blood,
the forgiveness of sins,
according to the riches of His grace which He made to abound
toward us in all wisdom and prudence."
—Ephesians 1:7–8

Chapter 4
A Special Purchase and Measuring Cup

*I*n order for the Master Chef to prepare and complete the sixty-six meals of the Word of God, a special purchase was made so that we could have this free dining experience. The Master Chef's main ingredient required this special purchase. To purchase means to acquire by payment; also, it means to redeem or obtain. *Redeem* denotes "to buy out," especially when purchasing a slave with respect to his or her freedom. Slaves, in biblical times, were released by a ransom price. The Master Chef paid that ransom price with His blood when He purchased us from the Slave Market of Sin (Exodus 21:30; Leviticus 25:48 and 51).

You see, our spiritual life story starts off with a spiritual exodus from Egypt. We were born trapped in an evil scheme by the slave master, Satan, to destroy us by throwing us in a deep, dark, empty pit of despair. We were abandoned, confused, and left there to die without any means of survival. We found ourselves spiritually kidnapped, sold, and held captive in this spiritually hostile place called "Spiritual Egypt" (the world as we know it).

In our bondage to Satan and sin, we experience famine because we are suffering from a great lack of spiritual food to keep us alive. In our lean, ugly state of mind, Jesus finds us. We have been slaving under sin, beaten down with guilt and shame, forced to labor in this sinful body. (Romans 7:14-25) The Pharaoh who reigns over us, Satan himself, constantly refuses to let us go. He nags and pulls at our hearts to stay with him so we will not follow our Savior, who wants to rescue us and lead us out of the wilderness of Sin and from our wilderness state of confusion into the Promised Land, flowing with the pure milk of grace and the sweet honey of mercy.

But our story does not end where it begins. It cost Jesus His life to pay the price for our freedom. However, our Redeemer is strong, and His name is the Lord of Hosts (Jeremiah 50:34). He vigorously pleaded our case to get a hold of us. His death on the cross is our only deliverance and freedom from the presence, power, and penalty of sin, and it has given us the opportunity to spend eternity with our new Master and Savior, who has adopted us into His holy family. (Read Romans 6) Here, we have received an inheritance. We are now free to taste the sweetness of His love and compassion from the fruits of the Tree of Life. We can dwell in the Promised Land, full of joy and peace, if we stop looking back and desiring what is on the table of Pharaoh and learn to enjoy dining at the banquet table overflowing with awesome delicacies to dine on with the King. "Now may the God of hope fill you with all joy and peace in believing, that you may abound in hope by the power of the Holy Spirit" (Romans 15:13).

The Master Chef, Jesus Christ, made a huge investment in our futures when He purchased us. Unlike some of us, who take chances and make financial investments with merely the hope of receiving a good return on our money, Jesus knew He was not taking a chance when He risked His life for us. But He also knew that it would be a bad investment if He didn't provide some type of assurance to protect it. He sent the Holy Spirit to abide in us, and in this way, He was *guaranteed* a good return once He made His purchase and returned home to take His rightful place next to our heavenly Father.

Jesus Christ purchased us by using His blood, which represents life. So in essence, when Jesus had shed His blood, He gave His life. Even though His blessings, His grace, His mercy, and His Word are free to us, the cost was by no means cheap, because "He gave

Himself as a ransom for all, the testimony borne at the proper time" (1 Timothy 2:6, NASB).

Since God is multi-rich in grace and extremely wealthy in mercy, He was the only One who could afford to pay the costly price to give us our freedom. And He invites us to dwell with Him now. The Most High God is the greatest Host, because He has the greatest abundance of provisions prepared for everyone who chooses to receive and accept Him.

Consider this through our culinary analogy for a moment. In gourmet cooking, accurate measurements are crucial to each meal. In order to keep the cost in line and ensure consistency in quality and quantity, ingredients and portions must be measured correctly each time. Nothing can be skimped on or overlooked. In our story, the Master Chef, Jesus Christ, used a special measuring cup called "The Cup of Salvation" to measure all the ingredients required to save each one who loves and accepts Him. He left nothing out of the measurements required to reconcile our relationship back to God, because these measurements were taken to the very extreme. In order to see what was really involved in dying the Master Chef had to taste these ingredients for Himself! Hebrews 2:9 "…because of the suffering of death crowned with glory and honor, that by the grace of God He might taste death for everyone." (NASB) It was the Father's will that the Master Chef fill His cup to the brim with extreme punishment, because the cup was prepared for a great many to be forgiven of their sins (Mark 14:36 – And He was saying, "Abba! Father! All things are possible for Thee; remove this cup from me; yet not what I will, but what Thou will." NASB)

Jesus's cup of betrayal, torture, and capital punishment was filled with the substances of humiliation, accusation, rejection, envy, jealousy, hatred, binding, scourging, mocking, stripping of garments, being spit on, a crown of thorns, beating, (sour) wine mixed with bitter gall, abuses, insults, denials, betrayals, cruelty, brutality, torture, insufferable thirst, agony, pain, starvation, stabbing, crucifying, and finally death. We could never have drunk from this cup and lived to tell about it. These ingredients were mixed together and placed in the Bread of Life to hang on the cross for our redemption.

Like every "meal" God serves us, redemption has several very important secret ingredients. One of the secret ingredients is forgiveness, which has freed us from the consequences of sin. He has also given us some natural herbs in our redemption: wisdom, which is seeing things from God's point of view to make decisions the way God would make them; providing us with the dietary fibers of knowledge and ability to discern what is right and what is wrong to live life well; and the spiritual herb of the desire to pursue understanding. Understanding gives us love for the will of God and clarity as to what is expected of us as His children. These herbs are important for spiritual digestive health.

Now that redemption has been fully prepared to the King's satisfaction, the Master Chef has also prepared a special cup for sinners to hold: the "Soup of Salvation," which they must dine on before they receive an invitation to dine properly at the King's banquet table. The "soup" is only offered to the poor and needy, because it holds all the ingredients for redemption.   Since Redemption is one of The Master Chef's specialties, He prepared this special soup Himself personally so that He could offer it to all who are willing to accept Him as their personal Lord and Savior.

Once you have accepted and dined on the Soup of Salvation, you will never be offered soup again, because you will have the privilege and luxury of dining from the royal table of the King, where you, prince or princess, will fine dine on divine selections of spiritual appetizers, salads, entrées, and desserts! Yes, *you can believe that it's butter* because according to Sous Chef Job, the Master Chef use what is real to smooth out our steps as we walk in His light through the darkened paths of this world. (Job 29: 3-6) The olive oil used to sauté the ingredients in the Master Chef's meals is the anointed oil of gladness (Hebrews 1:9b) You will also receive after-dinner mints of promises and sweet treats of blessings from the Master Chef to satisfy the spiritual hunger of every prince and princess in the royal kingdom of God. These specially prepared after-dinner mints and sweet treats are the Master Chef's way of saying "Thank You" for dining on His awesome delicacies prepared just for you.

These aspects of our redemption prove to us that the Master Chef, Jesus Christ, is awesome in the way He pours out His love and compassion for us! He has lavished His abundance of grace and mercy beyond measure, which we do not deserve, upon us so that we may be filled with spiritual knowledge to receive a full measure of the fullness of God. (1 Peter 1:2 "According to the foreknowledge of God the Father, by the sanctifying work of the Spirit, that you may obey Jesus Christ and be sprinkled with His blood: May grace and peace be yours in fullest measure." NASB)

Chapter 5

The Aged Royal Wine

"But the Helper, the Holy Spirit,
whom the Father will send in My name,
He will teach you all things, and bring to your remembrance
all things that I said to you."
—John 14:26

Chapter 5
The Aged Royal Wine

*I*n the culinary world, you will find that most chefs love to use wine in their dishes because wine adds a special flavor to the dish and also has the ability to break down the fat content in meat, which tenderizes it and makes it easier to chew and digest. As you feast on the Word of God, wine will be an essential part of every meal—but not the physical wine of this world. Rather, the Holy Spirit is the "Aged Royal Wine" that transports the nutrients of God's Word to each cell of the spiritual body and removes impurities from the bloodstream while repairing muscle damage caused by stubborn hardened arteries, increasing your blood supply, and strengthening the weakened vessels that flow to your heart. He cushions our joints, organs, and sensitive tissues to give us the strength to stand firm in difficult circumstances, as well as giving us the ability to perform at our fullest potential. The Holy Spirit puts pressure on our spiritual eyes' optic nerves so that we will acquire proper spiritual vision through God's light as He speaks to our minds and assists us according to the mind of Christ. He helps us become like Christ as we develop discernment in spiritual matters.

This Aged Royal Wine also helps to regulate the spiritual body's temperature as we endure the heat of trials and tribulations. It's important to realize that we must drink this wine daily, especially with every meal. Even though He never leaves us, it is best that we be filled with the Holy Spirit at all times as we face difficult and challenging situations and while studying the Word of God (John 14:26).

This wine will surely make your heart glad, because the Aged

Royal Wine is designed to make man's heart glad when he is walking in the power of the Holy Spirit (Psalm 104:15a). God would prefer that you not drink the physical wine that can make you drunk if you drink too much (Ephesians 5:18, NASB: "Do not get drunk with wine, for that is dissipation, but be filled with the Spirit"). But if we rely on the Holy Spirit to counsel and teach us in every situation, great or small, our hearts will be trouble free and safe from falling into sin. Fear will leave as you trust in the Holy Spirit, and peace will take residence to give you the confidence to endure while going through your tough times.

Not taking a full glass of the Aged Royal Wine with each meal will cause us to function way below our God-given potential. Trying to function spiritually without the Holy Spirit is like trying to survive without any food or drink.

The Holy Spirit is the mind of Christ in us. He is the powerful presence of God that abides in believers, gifting them for their perfection and enabling them to do the work of the ministry to edify the church body. The Holy Spirit has an amazing personality and role in our lives: He leads, indwells, empowers, anoints, intercedes, reveals, unifies, purifies, assures, illumines, guides, directs, gives evidence, warns, comforts, teaches, and gifts us. The indwelling of the Holy Spirit brings us into spiritual maturity.

Just as, in physical life, eating and drinking are not just done for their own sake—rather; they give us health, strength, and the ability to function as human beings—so it is spiritually. The Aged Royal Wine of the Holy Spirit is not only given to all of us for our enjoyment, but so that we can function as healthy, effective spiritual people. (1 Corinthians 12:13 "…and we were all made to drink of One Spirit." – NASB) A lifestyle of daily dining with the King and daily filling of the Spirit will lead to our discovery and use of God's gifts to us for the benefit of the whole body of Christ.

Ephesians 4:10 tells us that after Christ performed His great work on earth, He ascended far above all heavens to fill all things. When He did this, He gave spiritual gifts—gifts of the Holy Spirit— that are to accomplish three things: (1) the perfecting of the saints, (2) the work of the ministry, and (3) the edifying of the body of Christ, the church. Only those within the body of Christ receive spiritual gifts.

Spiritual gifts are empowered by the Holy Spirit and are graciously given to all of God's children for use in any ministry of the church. This includes gifts that are related to natural abilities, such as teaching, administration, or showing mercy and giving help to others. The gifts that appear miraculous, which are less related to natural abilities, include speaking in tongues, the interpretation of tongues, and the gifts of prophecy, healing, or discernment (1 Corinthians 12:30).

For the Holy Spirit to empower us simply means that He has the official authority to give us the resources and opportunities to work in ministry. In society, we are often faced with having the means without opportunity, or vice versa. Here, in the church of God's children, we have been given both the means and the opportunity to serve. This eliminates any excuse for not successfully performing the gifts that are within us (1 Corinthians 12:11 and 12:7).

Webster's New Collegiate Dictionary states that a gift is "something given, a talent of notable capacity; something voluntary that is transferred by one person to another without compensation. It is the act, right, or power of giving." Webster's definition even says that a gift *often implies special favor by God.* The spiritual gifts we receive are not earned or deserved, but are given based on God's grace. This means that we cannot pick and choose which gifts we want to operate in. Romans 12:4 states, "We have many members in one body, and all the members do not have the same function" (NASB). No two gifts are exactly the same; two people may have the same gift, but they will operate differently in it.

Romans 2:6 indicate that the Holy Spirit's gifts can be more or less strongly developed in different individuals or in the same individual over a period of time. That is why, in 1 Timothy 4:14, Paul reminded Timothy not to "neglect the gift that is in you." It was possible for his gift to weaken or go dormant due to infrequent use, and Paul wanted Timothy to stir his gift up and strengthen it during its usage. You can see how important it is to drink a full glass of the Aged Royal Wine—to be filled with the Holy Spirit—every day!

Let's break down each area of spiritual responsibility as outlined in Ephesians 4:10:

- *Perfecting the Saints:* It is implied that a saint will become flawless or complete in spiritual maturity. God promises to perfect the temple. Therefore, the growing perfection in you is a sign of God's supreme excellence and an indication of the unsurpassable accuracy of God's promises in Christ Jesus. God will complete His work of perfection in you as you use your spiritual gifts to His glory.
- *The Work of the Ministry:* The main object here is to *work.* It is the action required of every believer as he or she operates or functions by exerting strength or faculties to produce or perform various tasks or duties required in ministry while serving others in the church.
- *Edifying the Body of Christ:* The meaning of *edify,* in this case, is that the believer is to instruct or improve spiritually and in moral and religious knowledge as he or she assists in building and establishing the church body.

When we put the reasons for our gifting all together, we can see that spiritual gifts are for our benefit as well as for the benefit of others. God gives us spiritual gifts to perfect or complete us in spiritual maturity or excellence. The gifts function as we exert our strength or faculties to produce or to perform duties in the church. They improve us spiritually as well as improving our moral and religious knowledge as we build and establish the church.

The Master Chef wants to meet our needs, and He does so in the "Wine" that He serves: when we use our spiritual gifts, our needs are met. If everyone in the church uses his or her gifts to edify the body of Christ, then everyone's needs are met. God uses spiritual gifts to show believers, as well as the world, how much He loves us. It is our responsibility to use our spiritual gifts effectively and to seek to grow in them so that the church may receive the full benefit of the gifts over which the Master Chef has allowed us to be stewards. God is not a vending machine, where you can put in a few requests and select what you want from Him to get your needs met. If you have a need, plant a seed; and God will give you a harvest. It is out of your deep poverty that His generosity will provide you with good and plentiful crops.

God is faithful, and you can depend on Him to fulfill all of His promises; but you have to do what God has told you to do to get what He has promised to give you in return. The King has established ground rules and principles throughout His Word that we must live by if we want to be blessed and prosper in good health as well as in wealth.

First Corinthians 12:12 states, "For as the body is one, and has many members, but all the members of that one body, being many, are one body, so also is Christ." When we look at our physical bodies, we see that each part has a particular function. When all body parts are functioning properly, the result is a healthy body. In society, we consider people "handicapped" or "disabled" if they are missing a body part or if one just doesn't function properly. (Moreover, we don't just refer to one body part as handicapped, but the whole person!) When body parts that are essential for life are not functioning properly, death is imminent.

The same is true for the body of Christ. We have been ordained by God to use our spiritual gifts to edify the church and improve spiritually in building and establishing it. When we don't do this, the church becomes weak and dysfunctional because those members who are *not* using their spiritual gifts have disabled it. They may have even caused the death of an essential area of the church. When this happens, everyone in the church body suffers from this dysfunction.

No gift is too small to be included in this work. What if the mouth refused to eat? The entire body would suffer from the actions of one small part. As small as the mouth is, it can do great damage.

This is why it is so important that everyone uses his or her spiritual gifts to their fullest potential.

What spiritual gifts have been carried into *your* bloodstream by the Aged Royal Wine of the Holy Spirit? As you read the following list of spiritual gifts, consider fulfilling the desires that have been placed on *your* heart. (You can find these gifts listed in 1 Corinthians 7:7, 12:8–10, 28; Ephesians 4:11; Romans 12:6–8; and 1 Peter 4:11.)

Administration	Celibacy	Discernment
Encouragement Exhortation	Evangelism	Faith
Giving	Healing	Helps
Hospitality	Intercession	Interpretation of Tongues
Word of Knowledge	Leadership	Marriage
Mercy	Missionary Vocation	Miracles
Pastoring	Prophecy	Service
Teaching	Tongues	Word of Wisdom

One way you can seek for and identify your spiritual gifts is by looking for and asking about the needs and opportunities for ministry in your church. Our spiritual gifts are connected to the desires of our hearts, and God wants to fulfill those desires; they are also connected to the needs of the body of Christ. You can also do a self-examination to discover what interests, talents, and abilities you have that can be used to help build up the church body.

God's *gifts* to us have been specially wrapped in grace and are given to us to serve others. In exchange, our gift to God should be to embrace His gracious gift by making a commitment to Him and using our spiritual gifts (natural and supernatural) to work in ministry and edify the church body. We need to find out what our greatest desires are, match them up with the list of spiritual gifts, and then go and maximize them for God's glory. Don't forget to seal your gift to God in love, because those who have great spiritual gifts but "have not love" will profit nothing in God's sight (1 Corinthians 13:1–3).

The Holy Spirit is present to assist us in making good and

healthy decisions while using our gifts. Although it is not easy to learn good judgment—the ability to judge what is right and what is wrong is normally acquired throughout a lifetime of experience—it can also be accomplished through dining on meals of God's Word daily and relying on the Holy Spirit to guide us through this life. Good judgment is never completely mastered, but it is a goal toward which we should continually strive. Hebrews 6:4-5 "For in the case of those who have once been enlightened and have *tasted* of the heavenly gift and have been partakers of the Holy Spirit, and have *tasted* the good word of God and the powers of the age to come..." (NASB)

The Aged Royal Wine of the Holy Spirit is essential to our experiencing peace, joy, and victory in Christ as authentic Christians. God is not looking for us to be in a legalistic religion; He is looking for us to be in a loving relationship, for us to be real with Him—authentic and Christlike.

A Personal Recipe From
§ The Spiritual Gourmet Chef's Kitchen §

Are you thirsty?
Try this delicious drink recipe created by
your Spiritual Gourmet Chef.

Special Drink Recipe
Mt. Caramel Chocolate Shake

3 scoops vanilla ice cream
2 tablespoons Hershey's Chocolate Syrup
2 tablespoons caramel syrup
¼ teaspoon vanilla extract
¼ cup milk
¼ cup Carnation cream
¼ teaspoon Italian cream syrup (for sweetness)
Whipped cream
1 cherry

In the blender, mix all ingredients with the exception of the whipped cream and cherry. After blending the ingredients, pour into a sundae glass. Add a mountain of whipped cream and drizzle caramel syrup on top. Garnish your shake with a cherry on top.

A Mountain of Joy!

Chapter 6

Presentation:
The Master Chef's Sixty-Six Meals

"In the beginning was the Word, and the Word was with God,
and the Word was God.
He was in the beginning with God."
—John 1:1–2

"For the word of God is living and powerful,
and sharper than any two-edged sword,
piercing even to the division of soul and spirit,
and of joints and marrow, and is a discerner of the thoughts
and intents of the heart."
—Hebrews 4:12

Chapter 6
Presentation: The Master Chef's Sixty-Six Meals

God's great recipe book, the Bible, contains sixty-six distinct "meals," or books. Together, they contain enough fresh and nutritious spiritual food to last us a lifetime! God divinely inspired over forty Sous Chefs to assist Him in preparing these meals. It took thousands of years to express, exactly, the things that God wanted us to know about Him and His loving plans for us. Today, the meals are complete, and we are invited to dine.

The meals of God's Word are separated and presented to us in two major categories. The Old Testament books, of which there are thirty-nine, were originally written in Hebrew and were composed from about 1400 to 400 BC, which means it took approximately one thousand years to complete the various meals. The New Testament books, of which there are twenty-seven, were originally written in Greek and were composed from approximately AD 40 to AD 90. Between these two collections was a period of four hundred years of silence from God. The Bible gives a divine account of the origins of creation, unfolds the history of man, and tells us how God controls and cares about mankind. God also reveals His mighty power through these writings, especially when He called the whole universe into existence and commanded its order. The Bible fully informs us about the fall of mankind and God's provision for man's redemption. As you study, you will discover, throughout the Bible, God's grace and mercy for mankind. This grace is most purely reflected in His Son, Jesus Christ, who died on the cross and rose again with all power in His hand.

The Bible is built around the wonderful story of Christ and His promises of eternal life to all those who accept Him as their Lord and Savior. Jesus, who is God in the flesh, became a living sacrifice to give us a tangible vision and a perfect example of the kind of children He wants us all to become as we imitate and reflect the proper image of God (Ephesians 5:1–2: "Therefore, be imitators of God, as beloved children; and walk in love, just as Christ also loved you, and gave Himself up for us, an offering and a sacrifice to God as a fragrant aroma").

The Old Testament meals set the table for Christ's appearance, and the New Testament meals display and describe it. The Bible tells how Jesus planned for our redemption, died for our sins, rose from the dead, and lives today. It gives us this truth that we might believe, understand, know, love, give, and follow Him as His disciples as we go on this Great Commission as authentic Christians and spread the good news to the ends of the earth. Our Master Chef, Jesus Christ, is the *heart* and *center* of this great recipe book. Likewise, He should be the joyful heart and center of every believer of His Word.

The Master Chef has prepared these wonderful spiritual meals to reveal the truth which is found in Him, in His Word, and in His creation. As you dig in, you will soon have the desire to study more than thirty minutes a day. You will learn to identify the *genres,* or types of literature, in the Bible. You will learn how to analyze the facts and then classify those facts. More importantly, you will gain a deeper knowledge and closer relationship with God.

Sixty-Six Divinely Prepared Meals:
An Overview
Old Testament Meals
Thirty-Nine Books Written in Hebrew

Genesis	2 Chronicles	Daniel
Exodus	Ezra	Hosea
Leviticus	Nehemiah	Joel
Numbers	Esther	Amos
Deuteronomy	Job	Obadiah
Joshua	Psalms	Jonah
Judges	Proverbs	Micah
Ruth	Ecclesiastes	Nahum
1 Samuel	Song of Solomon	Habakkuk
2 Samuel	Isaiah	Zephaniah
1 Kings	Jeremiah	Haggai
2 Kings	Lamentations	Zechariah
1 Chronicles	Ezekiel	Malachi

Genesis: A Meal on the History of Creation

Genesis is the first meal in the great recipe book. It was prepared to describe creation, the origin and fall of man, and the corrupt, violent condition of man which caused God to send the Flood to cover the entire earth. The Flood was designed to destroy man and all his wickedness. However, God allowed one man whom He considered righteous to live, along with his family. The only living creatures to survive were Noah, his family, and the animals that entered the ark. This meal covers the creation week, the period from Adam to Abraham, and the formation of the twelve tribes of Israel.

Exodus, Leviticus, Numbers, and Deuteronomy: *Four Meals of Law*

The great Sous Chef, Moses, assisted the Master Chef in preparing these meals. This rich feast covers Israel's dramatic departure from Egypt and the giving of God's laws as He makes a covenant with His people, the Israelites.

Joshua, Judges, Ruth, 1 & 2 Samuel, 1 & 2 Kings, 1 & 2 Chronicles, Ezra, Nehemiah, and Esther: *Twelve Meals of History*

These meals display the faithfulness of God as He fulfills His promise to Abraham throughout, the history of the children of Israel as they enter the Promised Land and settle there. Because God's children wanted a king like those who had originally possessed the land, God honored their wishes and set up kings to rule over His children: first Saul, whose position was lost because of his rebellion against God, and then the psalmist David, the archetype of a godly king. The reign of David's son, King Solomon, follows. God considered Solomon the wisest man on earth, and he became greater than all the kings of the earth in riches and wisdom, yet he was foolish enough to marry seven hundred wives and princesses and three hundred concubines who turned his heart toward their gods (1 King 11:3). Then there is the division, apostasy, and decay of the kingdom, with a parallel description of two kingdoms: ten tribes that formed the Northern Kingdom, called Israel, and their destruction by Assyria; and the remaining two tribes that formed the Southern Kingdom, called Judah, and their captivity in Babylon. The history books open with the Hebrew nation in all its glory and close with the nation in ruins because of its sin and idolatry. They forgot that the Living God had saved them, and instead of remaining faithful, they chose to forsake the true King of kings.

Job, Psalms, Proverbs, Ecclesiastes, and the Song of Solomon:
Five Meals of Wisdom and Poetry These meals, full of spice and
sweetness, contain the direction of perfect, divine wisdom and
timeless principles to instruct us on how to enjoy the blessings of
successful godly living. Such guidance is compounded with superb
compositions of historical poetry and praise.

Isaiah, Jeremiah, Lamentations, Ezekiel, and Daniel: *Five Major
Prophets Meals*
These prophetic meals contain large portions of work by outstanding
Sous Chefs, prophets who were involved in the entire history of
Israel and provided them with a series of warnings, appeals for
repentance, messages of encouragement, visions of hope, and
assurances of restoration. These meals are sometimes sweet and
sometimes bitter, but they will aid you to grow as you look toward
the future.

***Hosea, Joel, Amos, Obadiah, Jonah, Micah, Nahum, Habakkuk,
Zephaniah, Haggai, Zechariah, and Malachi:*** *Twelve Minor
Prophets Meals*
These prophetic meals consist of smaller portions by the prophets,
who were also involved in the entire history of Israel, providing
them with visions of their future.

New Testament Meals

Twenty-Seven Books Written in Greek

Matthew	Ephesians	Hebrews
Mark	Philippians	James
Luke	Colossians	1 Peter
John	1 Thessalonians	2 Peter
Acts	2 Thessalonians	1 John
Romans	1 Timothy	2 John
1 Corinthians	2 Timothy	3 John
2 Corinthians	Titus	Jude
Galatians	Philemon	Revelation

Matthew, Mark, Luke, and John: *Four Meals on the Gospels of Christ*
These life-changing meals tell of the life of Christ while here on earth. They describe the life, death, and resurrection of Jesus Christ.

Acts: *A Meal on the History of the Church*
This historical meal was prepared by the Sous Chef Luke, who wrote of how the church was born and told of its early days and the spread of Christianity after the ascension of Christ.

The Epistles: *Twenty-One Meal Recipes for Christian Life and Doctrine*
<u>Thirteen of the epistles</u>—that is, letters—were prepared by the Sous Chef Paul, the Master Chef's assistant missionary to the Gentiles. Romans, 1 & 2 Corinthians, Galatians, Ephesians, Philippians, Colossians, 1 & 2 Thessalonians, 1 & 2 Timothy, Titus, and

Philemon are also referred to as *the Pauline Epistles.*

The other *eight epistles*—Hebrews, James, 1 & 2 Peter, 1, 2, & 3 John, and Jude, were prepared by various other Sous Chefs to meet specific needs that Paul could not meet. All of these meals were prepared for particular reasons and address churches or individuals. The epistles mainly deal with doctrinal issues and how the church and family should properly function as believers.

Revelation: One Meal of Prophecy

Revelation is the last meal in the great recipe book of God. This prophetic meal describes the church age, the coming tribulation period, and the second coming of Christ and His new order. It describes how the age will end and what is yet to come. This new order consists of the Thousand-Year Kingdom of Christ here on earth and then the final destruction and replacement of the heavens and earth with what is called "the New Heavens and the New Earth" (Revelation 21:1).

It is good practice to memorize the names of the books of the Bible and become familiar with them. When you are familiar with the genres of Scripture, you'll be better able to identify the book a particular Scripture was taken from, and you will have a better overview of the entire feast of the sixty-six meals.

Chapter 7

You Are What You Eat, Drink and Think

"For he who eats and drinks in an unworthy manner eats and drinks judgment to himself, not discerning the Lord's body."
—1 Corinthians 11:29

Chapter 7
You Are What You Eat, Drink, and Think

*T*he meals of God's Word are best served sit-down-dinner style, and not as a buffet where you *"Dip and Skip"*. Buffets are the favorite of picky eaters: they give opportunity to pick and choose what looks good to them. Unfortunately, Christians do the same thing when it comes to reading and listening to the Word of God. Some Christians want to focus only on those things they prefer to hear and know. To dip into what they like and skip what they don't like is not beneficial to any believer. You end up only dealing with those things that make you feel good, as opposed to what is actually good for you.

The whole point of dining on spiritual meals is to develop Christlike characteristics. What you spiritually eat and drink affects your thinking. Proverbs 23:7 says: "For as he thinks within himself, so he is. He says to you eat and drink." (NASB) And in order to live right, we must first *think* right. Our lives are the product of our thoughts. What you believe about God determines your attitude and behavior toward Him. If we read and study the Bible frequently, God's thoughts will eventually become our thoughts, and His ways will transform our ways. The end result is that we will be transformed into His image.

Eat Fresh

God has provided so much fresh food for each of us to feast on, so why are we always eating off of someone else's plate? Why would we eat only leftovers or pre-chewed food? That's what happens when we get all of our exposure to the Word from sermons at church, or from testimonies and Christian literature. We are digesting what someone else ate, never discovering firsthand what the food really tastes like.

Back in the day, as babies were weaned off milk, mothers would chew the baby's food and then take it out of their mouths and place it into the baby's mouth. Some of the original flavors from the food remained in the mother's mouth, so what she gave her child was distorted, diluted, and mixed with the juices from her mouth. The baby had no way of knowing how the food had originally tasted. As babies got older, they were spoon-fed for a period of time and eventually began to feed themselves.

Just as babies start off on milk and grow up to eat solid foods, so babes in Christ should be maturing. It is natural to be on the milk of God's Word at first and to go through this stage of growing because milk is the elementary teachings of Christ. (1 Peter 2:2: "As newborn babies, desire the pure milk of the word that you may grow thereby, if indeed you have tasted that the Lord is gracious"). It is natural, too, to be spoon-fed bite by bite for a period of time— sermons and testimonies have their place! But God wants His children to grow up, be weaned off of milk, and get to a stage where we can eat solid foods on our own, with the ability and strength to feed ourselves by handling His Word rightly. He wants us to know firsthand how to deal with life according to His purposes.

In order for us to become mature in Christ, God has called us to learn how to chew our own food without relying on someone else to chew up the food first or spoon-feed it to us. There's a danger here besides that of remaining immature: relying always on someone else to teach us the Word of God puts us in danger of receiving distorted food that contains the personal flavors of that individual's taste, which dilute and even change the original flavors that *God* prepared and intended us to taste for ourselves. Hebrews 5:13-14 "For everyone who partakes only of milk is not accustomed to the word of righteousness for he is a babe. But solid food is for the mature, who because of practice have their senses trained to discern good and evil." (NASB) God wants all of His children eventually weaned off of breast-milk and ready to give up their immature childish ways so they can pick up a spiritual knife (the Bible) and a spiritual fork (the concordance) and begin cutting into, eating, and digesting the meat of the Word every day. This way they don't have to wait to eat once a week as they dine on a Sunday sermon, but they can keep the Word fresh in their hearts and minds as they eat fresh from the King's banquet table every day.

The Knowledge of the Truth of God and the Lies of Satan

There are three levels of the knowledge of God: what we *know,* what we *believe,* and what we *don't know.* God has created a great feast called the Bible because He will not have any of His children ignorant of the truth about Himself and His plans for them to spend eternity with Him. God wants His loved ones to operate on the level of *knowing.* Unfortunately, a great many of His children operate on the last two levels only, because we don't take the time to study God's precious Word to know the truth. The greatest tragedy for us, as God's children, is that Satan also operates at his best within these two areas. He knows that we don't really know the truth like we should. So how does he deceive us?

First of all, while God is all truth and 100 percent of truth is found in Christ Jesus, if *any* percentage of a lie is added to the truth of the Word of God, it is no longer the truth. A half-twisted truth becomes a totally straight lie. We tend to believe lies that have been mixed with the truth because we don't know the whole truth and nothing but the truth.

If this sounds familiar, it should. It's the same trick Satan used on Eve in the Garden of Eden when he mixed the truth with a lie. Since the command not to eat from the Tree of the Knowledge of Good and Evil was given directly to Adam before Eve was formed, Eve may have been speaking what she only believed. Could Eve have been operating on what she thought she had heard—perhaps from Adam—as opposed to what she knew to be the truth?

In any case, Eve had every opportunity to go straight to God to find out exactly what the truth was concerning the tree in the middle of the garden. We have the same opportunity through prayer and the Word. We don't have to go *to* or *through* anyone else to get to the truth about the Tree of Life that sits in the middle of our lives.

When you operate on the level of what you *know,* you have personal knowledge—based on your own study, research, or experience—to back you up.

True knowledge of Jesus will take you past the greatest general knowledge of Christ as the world's Savior, of His virgin birth and how He died in our place and rose again after three days. True knowledge of Christ will take you to an intimate, passionate place where you come to know why Christ is your Savior and chose to die in your place. Time spent intimately with Him every day will give you those personal experiences of His love and compassion for you.

It is very difficult for anyone, including Satan, to deceive you when you have experience and real knowledge behind you. This is why God didn't tell us to *listen* to His Word or *read* His Word to show ourselves approved unto Him, but to *study.* God wants us to acquire firsthand knowledge. When we know and go to the source of truth, we are safeguarded from receiving the truth mixed with lies or being ignorant, confused, or deceived by Satan. And just as physical food will keep you alive, solid spiritual food will keep you from being destroyed due to lack of knowledge (Hosea 4:6).

When you operate just on the level of what you *believe,* you are living based on what you have learned, been taught, or heard from someone else. In other words, you're operating in secondhand knowledge. You haven't acquired personal knowledge, nor do you have any way of validating the information to prove that what you believe is really true. Generally, you don't even know the original source of the information you have received. You can be made to believe a lie without knowing it is one, and you become susceptible to Satan's deceptions unless you take the necessary steps to study a thing out for yourself.

The last level is what we *don't know.* Here, there is no personal knowledge or experience of God's Word to defeat the lies of Satan, who is the father of lies. On this level, we don't even have a steady diet of secondhand truth. If you have no knowledge of the truth, you're in a very dangerous position. God said, "My people are destroyed for lack of knowledge" (Hosea 4:6). You are destroyed by lack of knowledge because you are *rejecting* knowledge which would free you from your ignorance in not personally knowing who God is. Those who are content to remain in the realm of not-knowing are vulnerable to all of Satan's deceptive, lying schemes to kill, steal from, and destroy them.

The Master Chef Jesus had Sous Chef Jeremiah plainly prepare one of the entrées to say this: that you are not wise and will be put to shame when you don't know the ordinance of the Lord (see Jeremiah 8:7-10). If you reject His Word, then what kind of wisdom will you have? You are operating under ignorance and practicing deceit because you have allowed yourself to be deceived, and your understanding has become superficial. It appears that we must dumb down our ignorance and wise up on truth in order to know the Lord and His Word for ourselves!

To get a clearer vision of this, look at Daniel 10:3, where Sous Chef Daniel said, "I did not eat any tasty food, nor did meat or wine enter my mouth." You see, false religion's food should not taste good to you at all, because it is defiled and unclean meat prepared from lies. It is the food of our greatest Enemy. According to Daniel 11:26-27, those who eat the choice food of their enemies will be destroyed by them because they speak lies to each other at the same table. Unlike the Lord of Hosts, who is the perfect Host, the false religions are bad hosts because their houses are unclean, and everything in them is filthy. Their only knife (book) is dirty, because they cut up the meat of all their lies with that same knife. Their hands are very filthy from lies, and yet they still serve you, allowing you to eat from their filthy hands because they don't possess a fork that they can use to prove that they are feeding you the truth.

Moreover, if you refuse to know God and His Word, then you are truly dining on the stubbornness of your heart (Jeremiah 13:10: "This wicked people, who refuse to listen to My words, who walk in the stubbornness of their hearts"). You are reflecting the characteristics of an atheist when you call yourselves Christians but act or behave like God does not exist.

You see, Satan knows the Word of God better than some of us. He can change one little word and have a believer who has not personally studied God's Word believe a lie about Jesus and His Word. With the help of Satan, many of the cults and false religions have taken some of God's truths and mixed them with their personal twist. When we hear them quote their version of their "so-called" truth, some of us buy into the lie (just like Eve did) because it sounds so similar to what we have heard. In order to detect the *"genuine"* Word of God from the *"fake"* prophets and their religions you must learn to recognize the differences and not focus on the similarities because they are using the truth to mix with their lies so they can deceive you and draw you away from the real truth found only in Jesus Christ and His Word. You must learn to "BYOB"- Bring Your Own Bible and read from it.

Furthermore, God doesn't want any of His children visiting their houses to listen to or dine on their lies about Him. Jeremiah 16:8 says, "Moreover you shall not go into a house of feasting to sit with them to eat and drink." Now watch this: God prepared it best in *Proverbs 14:15,* "The naïve believe everything," but in *Proverbs 15:14 He* says, "The mind of the intelligent seeks knowledge." Did you catch the use of proverbs? God is so amazing; see how the numbers were reversed so we can visualize God's true vision for us! You can reverse your ignorance when you understand that in order to be spiritually intelligent, you simply need to seek God by studying His Word to gain knowledge and wisdom, and then you will know for yourself what to believe and who to believe in everything. In other words, stay in God's house and dine only from His table if you want the whole truth as you feast on the Word of God and drink the Aged Royal Wine; allowing them only to *"Wine and Dine You".*

God has instructed us to be transformed by the renewing of our minds (Romans 12:2). When our minds are transformed in the ways and teachings of Christ, Satan can no longer deceive us as he used to do. The old tricks just won't work on us anymore, because the old man has become a new creature. "The old things have passed away; behold, new things have come" (2 Corinthians 5:17). Of course, don't get this twisted . . . the old creature is still hanging around to see if he or she can get back in. That's when you give Satan a chance to try new schemes in hopes of finding you empty of the Spirit. He might try to get you to go for what is *good,* for example, instead of what is *best* for you. But if we continually study God's Word to renew our minds through the drinking of the Holy Spirit, God will keep us from stumbling over half-truths and falling for Satan's lies.

God has our best interests at heart. He desires the best for all of His children. We must learn how to go after the best that God has for us and not settle for anything less.

Chapter 8

The Basics of Spiritual Nutrition

*"For no one ever hated his own flesh, but nourishes and cherishes it,
just as the Lord does the church. For we are members of His body,
of His flesh and of His bones."*
—Ephesians 5:29–30

Chapter 8
The Basics of Spiritual Nutrition

*P*raise and worship are like spiritual vitamins and supplements that dissolve throughout the spiritual body. "God is Spirit, and those who worship Him must worship in spirit and truth" (John 4:24). Vitamins help to support our vision and hearing. Supplements are known for their nutritional and healthy effects on the joints, giving us mobility and maximum flexibility. They are critical for the proper release of energy in our bodies, and they keep our active lifestyles going strong. Praise and worship act much the same way in our spiritual lives. They enable us to see clearly and hear from God, and they keep us active and energetic as we serve Him.

These *personally prescribed* spiritual vitamins and vitamin supplements help to boost the spiritual immune system and protect against heart disease, which is caused by a lack of the Word to protect the heart and help against Satan's cancerous diseases. They are the *prescribed* praises and worship of God that are found in His Word, which you can take and use to *personally* praise and worship God for yourself.

As Christians, we often verbally express our love for the Lord, but it is our attitude toward the Bible that indicates our true attitude toward Christ. (Jeremiah 12:3 tells us, "But thou knowest me, O Lord; thou seest me; and thou dost examine my heart's attitude toward thee.") Since the Aged Royal Wine, the Holy Spirit, contains all of the elements of the Fruit of the Spirit, then drinking a full glass of this fruit drink will have great effect on our attitudes. To show true love for the Lord means we must allow the Holy Spirit to change our appetites, our behaviors, and the condition of our hearts as He teaches us how to love God through the grace of Jesus Christ. Scripture says that "Those who love Me will keep My commandments" (John 14:15, 21; see also Deuteronomy 5:10 and Exodus 20:6).

Praise and worship are essential for the nourishment, energy, and growth of our spiritual lives. They are a natural part of our lives only when we digest the Word of God daily. Applying the Word of God will help to control any spiritual disorders that may arise when you are exposed to deception, lies, and sinful behavior and activity. Romans 10:17 tells us that faith comes from hearing the Word of God. It's the Word of God that will feed your hunger and increase your appetite for more. When you seek God and find Him in His Word, you will begin to digest the truths there, and the resulting praise will then change your mindset. The more you dine, the greater your appetite will become because of the cravings you will develop as you seek God. The Word of God also provides the wisdom of knowing who God is because it will show you His works and the reasons you should praise Him. As you digest these vitamins and supplements daily, you will find yourself naturally worshiping the God you are learning about!

Praise and worship flow out of our knowledge and love for God; which are developed as we dine at the King's table. The meals we find in the Word could be said to contain several vitamins which build praise and worship into our lives:

Vitamin A = *Appetite:* Provides a desire and hunger for the Word of God.

> We desire truth in the innermost being and in the hidden part. It makes us acquire wisdom. (Psalm 51:6)

Vitamin B = *Behavior:* Instructions for us to conduct ourselves in wise behavior.

> To receive instruction in wise behavior. (Proverbs 1:3)

> But as He who called you is holy, you also be holy in all your conduct, because it is written, Be holy, for I am holy. (1 Peter 1:15)

Vitamin C = *Condition:* Conditions our hearts in faith to take God at His Word.

> A joyful heart is good medicine. (Proverbs 17:22, NASB)

> Your word I have hidden in my heart, that I may not sin against You. (Psalm 119:11)

> Let the words of my mouth and the meditation of my heart be acceptable in Your sight, O Lord, my strength and my Redeemer. (Psalm 19:14)

The Proteins for Holiness, Godliness, and Righteousness

Each meal in God's Word is full of rich "proteins," components of the Word that God provides for His children to guarantee their holiness and righteousness in Him. These spiritual proteins are extremely complex in nature, and they complete the believer. The combinations of proteins consist of all nine essential elements found in the Fruit of the Spirit: *love, joy, peace, patience, kindness, goodness, faithfulness, gentleness,* and *self-control* (Galatians 5:22–23). These are the superb qualities that produce godliness because they cause us to resemble our Lord and Savior. However, they are only complete when we use them all together to produce holiness and righteousness in Christ.

Spiritually, just as physically, proteins increase our metabolism and help produce healthy spiritual muscles, organ tissues, and bones. Proteins play a vital role in strengthening the immune system and help build spiritual muscles. Dining on the Word of God will pump these proteins into your life and kick-start your own transformation into the likeness of God!

Proteins for Holiness

> So that He may establish your hearts blameless in holiness before our God and Father at the coming of our Lord Jesus Christ with all His Saints. (1 Thessalonians 3:13)

Proteins for Godliness

> . . . that we may lead a quiet and peaceable life in all godliness and reverence. For this is good and acceptable in the sight of God our Savior who desires all men to be saved and to come to the knowledge of the truth. (1 Timothy 2:2–4)

Proteins for Righteousness

> He restores my soul; He guides me in the paths of righteousness for His name's sake. (Psalm 23:3)
> All discipline for the moment seems not to be joyful, but sorrowful; yet to those who have been trained by it, afterwards it yields the peaceful fruit of righteousness. (Hebrews 12:11)

Chapter 9

Food and Dining Safety

*"But the Lord is faithful, who will establish you
and guard you from the evil one."*
—2 Thessalonians 3:3

Chapter 9
Food and Dining Safety

$\mathcal{T}$he importance of food safety cannot be emphasized enough. Spiritual food-borne illnesses exist which are detrimental to the believer and are usually carried into our spiritual bodies by sinful thoughts, speech, and actions. Through regular consumption of His divinely prepared meals, God has provided protection for us from this deadly problem. However, handlers of the Word of God must use the proper methods and utensils to consume the Word properly. Dining at the spiritual dinner table is not always a perfectly precise art, but knowledge of the basics will help you take in the greatest nourishment.

Most of us know that God has a plan for our lives, which is based on the principles of His Word. But do you know that Satan also has a master plan for your life which is opposite to God's plan for you? Satan's plan for your life is set up to kill, steal from, and destroy you through the principles of his deception: he uses lies that appear to be truths to seduce you into thinking that some of the dangerous things you see, taste, smell, feel, hear, and believe are good, when the truth is they are not good for you at all.

Satan's plans are structured to dispute God's Word, question God's love, and finally have us reject the Word of God entirely. When we do not know the truth of Scripture for ourselves, we'll often find ourselves making the very same mistakes Eve made while in the Garden of Eden. She subtracted from God's Word and questioned His love, grace, and authority. Then she *added* to God's Word and changed it by misquoting Him (Genesis 3:3). She fell right into Satan's master plan, and it killed her spiritually. Her right to eternal life, without experiencing physical death, was stolen. Her chance of living in the Garden of Eden forever was destroyed, and her walk with God was demolished, all because of a lie that appeared to her as the truth.

To keep us from making the same mistakes, each word in God's great recipe book, the Bible, has been prepared with rich ingredients to fill us up with spiritual knowledge. These meals will stimulate our minds so we can develop the art of asking the right questions and finding the right answers for ourselves when we go straight to the truth.

Spiritual Food-Borne Illnesses

Spiritual food-borne illnesses are caused by digesting *perverted, adulterated,* and *fornicated* half-truths that are contaminated with spiritual viruses, parasites, and bacteria: those unseen "principalities . . . powers . . . rulers of the darkness of this age . . . [and] spiritual hosts of wickedness in heavenly places" that are sent by Satan to attack the weak parts of our spiritual immune systems with his "free radicals" of temptation (Ephesians 6: 11b-12). Free radicals are the unstable and highly reactive schemes Satan tempts you with that can damage the spiritual body because they accelerate the progression of spiritual cancer and cardiovascular diseases that affect your heart.

The severity of illness will depend to a great extent on the Christian's susceptibility. We need to build up our spiritual immune systems, which are always under attack by Satan. If we listen to lies and practice sin in our lives, these elements of our "diets" will open the door to spiritual illnesses. Generally, illnesses will have a greater difficulty in being effective if we dine daily on healthy spiritual food and regularly praise and worship God, which is like taking a personally prescribed, daily dose of spiritual vitamins and vitamin supplements! The meals of the Bible are designed to trim and keep the fat off of us so we can stay healthy and strong in the Lord. Some meals in the Word are designed to detoxify our systems, getting rid of the sin in our former diets. These meals prepare our spirits for holiness and righteousness.

Food safety is of great concern to the Master Chef. He has gone to great lengths to ensure that the quality and quantity of food He has provided will be ample for us. Nothing but the best has been given to nourish the spiritual bodies of His children. He put His own life at stake to assure that safe and wholesome food would be served to all of His children in a safe and secure environment. But we must stay in the Word and dine on God's meals to stay safe and secure from becoming weak and sickly.

Chapter 10

Daily Spiritual Food Guide Pyramid

*"This is the bread which came down out of heaven-
not as your fathers ate the manna, and are dead.
He who eats this bread will live forever."*
—John 6:58

Chapter 10
Daily Spiritual Food Guide Pyramid

*T*he Daily Spiritual Food Guide Pyramid presents the recommended daily food intake for an optimum spiritual life. It shows the health benefits of a balanced diet and illustrates the dietary requirements for all age groups. The food groups have different functions and focuses, but they all help the believers eat well and live better.

Following the balanced diet recommended in the pyramid will reduce or prevent spiritual diseases that destroy our hearts. Recommended servings may vary depending on each believer's spiritual requirements—the servings suggested should be a *minimum* part of your daily diet.

The great thing about this spiritual diet is that you can eat as much as you want and not have to worry about getting fat! The Master Chef's food is so healthy that the more you eat, the better you will look and feel.

Daily Spiritual Food Guide Pyramid

(The Basic Six Spiritual Food Groups)

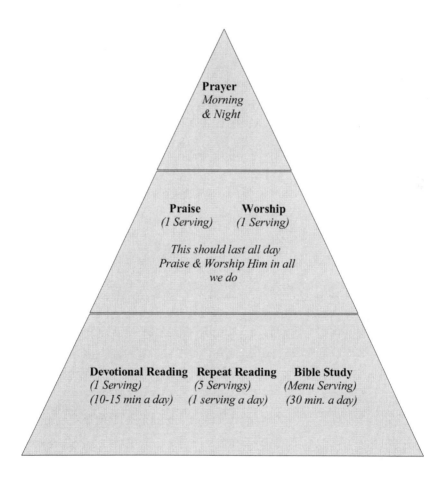

Prayer
Morning
& Night

Praise **Worship**
(1 Serving) *(1 Serving)*

This should last all day
Praise & Worship Him in all
we do

Devotional Reading **Repeat Reading** **Bible Study**
(1 Serving) *(5 Servings)* *(Menu Serving)*
(10-15 min a day) *(1 serving a day)* *(30 min. a day)*

The Daily Spiritual Food Guide Pyramid has been broken down into six basic food groups:

Food Group 1: Prayer

Prayer is simply addressing or conversing directly with God. Prayer may be silent or spoken aloud, but either way, it is speaking straight from the heart. Prayer pours out what is in your soul before the Lord, showing that you believe in His personality, ability, and willingness to help you, and that you know He has total control of all things. A minimum of two servings a day should be in your daily diet. Prayer can be formal (bowing your knees, closing your eyes, bowing your head, and folding your hands together with a formal introduction), or it can be informal (just talking to God whenever, however, and wherever you are). Prayer can be spoken in secret or in public, occasionally or constantly. It can be a simple conversation, a song, a crying out, or a moan. However you communicate with God, you must be sincere, offering up your prayers with reverence and godly fear, in humbleness and in faith. Without expressing any doubt in your heart or mind, you must believe that God will hear and answer your prayers, fulfilling His Word, as He promised that if you ask, you shall receive (Matthew 7:7–8).

Prayer should be offered in the name of Jesus to keep down any confusion as to whom you are praying. Take it from the prophet Elijah: "Then you call on the name of your gods, and I will call on the name of the LORD; and the God who answers by fire, He is God" (1 Kings 18:24). Elijah knew God because he had personal knowledge due to his conversations with God. As he obeyed God's Word, he experienced God's sovereignty (1 Kings 17).

God knows that there are those of us who struggle with doubt in our hearts and minds concerning Him. If you are struggling with doubt because you feel that God does not hear or answer your prayers, then read what God says in Mark 9:23: "If you can? Everything is possible for one who believes" (NIV). Learn from the man who also struggled with that same problem, but who immediately exclaimed, "I do believe! Help me overcome my unbelief." Remember, when we are weak, then our faith in God is what is needed to connect to God's strength. But according to Sous Chef Mark, in Mark 9:24, it's up to you to make the connection. "If you can!" So I say to you, like Jesus said to this man, *"if you can,"* just ask God to help your unbelief and "believe that He can" do what's impossible for you to do alone.

Learn to season God's food with your prayers. The seasoning used in one's prayers becomes a sweet, savory flavor that produces a sweet aroma to the King while at the dinner table, giving God the opportunity to help you with whatever doubts you have about Him and His Word.

Food Group 2: Praise

To praise is to commend or sing to the Lord. True praise is an inward emotion—a gladness and rejoicing of the heart, or a music of the soul and spirit. It is our duty to praise God. Moreover, praise should be a natural impulse—as well as a delight—for every believer. To fail in our duty to praise God is to withhold from God that which rightfully belongs to Him. When we praise God, we give Him the honor, glory, and gratitude we owe Him, so we need to cultivate an attitude of praise and get into the habit of doing it every day. It should be a desire and a delight to look for reasons to praise God.

Reasons to praise God can be found all throughout the Bible. Every breath we take is just one of many reasons to praise Him! Scripture commands, "Everything that has breath, praise the Lord" (Psalm 150:6).

Praise benefits us as well, as is seen in the earlier section on spiritual vitamins. It empowers us, strengthens us, and keeps our focus on the Lord so that His energy and holiness can pour through our lives. This is also true of worship.

Food Group 3: Worship

Worship can be done individually or corporately, in private or in public. "They that worship Him, worship in Spirit and Truth" because God is Spirit (John 4:23–24). We will not find God in any idol or statue made by man. (In Acts 17:29 it reads "Being then the offspring of God, we ought not to think that the Divine Nature is like gold or silver or stone, an image formed by the art and thought of man. And in Acts 19:26 "...saying that gods made with hands are no gods at all." – NASB) To be truthful, we are required to worship the Creator, not His creation. (Romans 1:25 says "For they exchanged the truth of God for a lie, and worshiped and served the creature rather than the Creator, who is blessed forever. Amen" – NASB) You'll find that worship is far deeper than just emotion or even the surrendering of the will. Worship can appear different from praise because, while praise is expressed mainly in words, worship is expressed in our actions as well. Praise thanks God for what He has done, and worship adores Him for who He is.

Regular dining on the Word of God will inform both our worship and our praise: we can use God's words to find many reasons to praise Him, and we can also use God's words to instruct our actions, attitude, and behavior to worship Him in everything we do, say, and think. Both should give glory to God. Worship is beyond our own efforts as well: it is a response of God's Spirit in us to the Spirit in Him. It is a great way to connect with God and express our gratitude to Him as we "kiss" Him with worship.

Food Group 4: Devotional Reading

Devotional reading, sometimes called "quiet time," is a quiet time, in a quiet place, for a quiet heart to hear the still small voice of God as He quietly speaks to give direction and counsel. It is a time set, preferably in the morning, to just read God's love letters (the Bible) back to Him. It is a special time when you can be alone with God to respond to Him, expressing how you feel and receiving special direction or a message from Him before you start your busy day. It's also a time when God has your undivided attention and speaks to you directly through His Word when you need an answer to a prayer, to fulfill a hunger or desire of the heart, or to give you a blessing from His Word that will benefit you later in the day. Its quiet light will glow throughout your day, which is why this book often refers to quiet time as "Royal Candlelight Devotional Moments" with God.

A regular devotional reading habit will help disciples to develop a regular study habit. As you spend time with God reading His Word, you will began to have questions about what you are reading, which will require you to study to get the answers to your questions. You will find out that God will answer some of your questions only through studying.

This is also a good time to keep your special notebook or Your Daily Bread Spiritual Journal handy to write down any thoughts or answers from God that are expressed during this time. You can sit with the expectation that God is going to speak to you and give you a visional sign or evidence that will strengthen your faith in Him. God always speaks through His Word. There will be times while you are studying when God's Word will clearly speak directly to you regarding a situation in your life. His Word will give you a sign and the evidence you need to trust in Him as He shows you that He is working on your behalf.

Devotional reading is a great opportunity to learn and apply God's principles, which are profitable for every believer. The basic principles to live by can be found in Proverbs, which is a meal full of timeless wisdom that can be read devotionally every day. Proverbs contains thirty-one chapters, each one a spiritual "breakfast bar" packed with wisdom, energy, joy, and instruction for life, with a sweet treat attached—a promise of a blessing to lengthen our lives if we obey its teachings.

Try spending a Royal Candlelight Moment to read a devotional chapter before going about your busy day. It's not advisable to wait until later in the day, as many distractions are liable to come up and restrict your special time with God.

Food Group 5: Repeat Reading

Repeat reading involves reading a particular Scripture you have decided to study to allow God to reveal the mysteries of His Word. Quite often, you will find that each time you read the same Scripture, God will reveal something different, based on your spiritual needs at the time. This is God's way of speaking to His children to teach and guide them through various areas of their lives.

Food Group 6: Bible Study

Bible study is your opportunity to dine! It is now that you can truly dig into the Royal Candlelight Thirty-Minute Meals with God. Thirty minutes a day in the study of God's Word is a quick and easy routine for getting into God's Word for yourself. Bible study is a great opportunity to allow the Holy Spirit to operate in your life, teaching you what God has to say about every area of your life and preparing you to deal with various situations that you will face.

Second Timothy 2:15 tells us that God expects us to study to show ourselves approved unto Him and to be able to rightly divide His Word of truth. We can only achieve this goal through regular reading and studying.

However, studying God's Word is different from just *reading* His Word. Bible study involves questions and answers. You can write your questions down and then ask God to reveal the answers to you while you are studying. God, in His generous nature, states in His Word that all we have to do is ask, and He will give us the knowledge and understanding required to know Him (James 1:5: "But if any of you lacks wisdom, let him ask of God, who gives to all men generously and without reproach, and it will be given to him"). Understanding God's Word will come as you study and diligently seek Him. No study, no understanding.

Although God sometimes speaks into our lives when we're not expecting it, we must not assume that God is always going to speak to us without our making an effort to seek Him for wisdom, knowledge, and understanding. The understanding of His Word will come through a continual and consistent study of His Word. This is a basic principle of relationship: we cannot get to know those we do not spend time with or listen to. The more you seek God for an understanding of who He is the better or closer your relationship will be, and the more God will reveal Himself to you.

A minimum of one hour a day should be routinely devoted to being in the presence of God to serve up prayer, praise, worship, reading, and study, which are all forms of thanksgiving to the Master Chef. God deserves to be worshiped, thanked, and praised every day!

You can serve up prayer, praise, and worship together in a minimum of fifteen minutes, based on the overall time you wish to spend in the presence of God. In following the Daily Spiritual Food

Guide Pyramid, you can create your own recipes for devotional reading, repeat reading, and Bible study.

Chapter 11

Making Your Dinner Reservations for Two

"I have set the LORD always before me;
Because He is at my right hand I shall not be moved."
—Psalm 16:8

Chapter 11
Making Your Dinner Reservations for Two

*W*e have already seen that our Master Chef has put untold hours, effort, and expertise into preparing spiritual meals for us from the best of ingredients. When it comes time to dine, then, we should not expect to rush through and enjoy His meals without spending hours, effort or attention. (After all, you wouldn't treat a French chef's masterpiece like "junk food", would you?) Dining on God's meals requires hard mental work; however, the rewards are astounding. The spiritual food of God's Word is designed and prepared to have a dramatic impact on our lives.

At times it may seem that no matter how long you linger over your spiritual dinner, the time is not long enough. Be encouraged: stay focused on the goal so that you can make the best possible use of the time you have to dine on spiritual meals each day. Dining on the Word should be a part of your daily routine, just like physically eating and drinking . . . and we all like to take time to do this.

Sometimes we are tempted to kick against this requirement. We'd rather eat fast food. But think about the efforts we make in other areas of lives. We make all types of appointments to accomplish various tasks. We have a set time to work, and we schedule time for vacations or relaxation, appointments and meetings. In your scheduling, set aside a time just for meeting and relaxing with God, alone, on a regular, ongoing basis. Make daily dinner reservations for two, and spend *at least* thirty minutes dining on spiritual food every day with the King.

If you look over your present schedule, you can probably see where you waste a lot of precious time through long conversations on the telephone, watching hours of television, sleeping long hours, or reading materials other than the Bible. What about long periods of shopping till you drop, or other things you consider important to you? You, like most of us, probably spend a lot of time on such pursuits. Yet, let's be honest: when it comes to spending time with our Savior, we immediately feel that we don't have the time. On the contrary; we *do* have the time, because God has given us plenty of time to spend with Him if we have the desire to do so.

Invest some time in evaluating your daily routine. Besides the thirty minutes you'll take to study for "dinner," prioritize your day to include time in the morning to sit in the presence of God and do some devotional reading of the Bible. Devotional reading (also known as "quiet time," or in this book, "Royal Candlelight Devotional Moments") is considered *devotional* because you are focused on God as the object of worship, and you are taking the necessary steps to create an atmosphere of praise and worship to Him. This is so important before starting off on your busy day! This is a time when God has an opportunity to share a personal word with you through His Word. Make a daily appointment to personally meet and fellowship with God through prayer, worship, and Bible reading. Then schedule at least thirty minutes a day on top of that for studying God's Word.

Scheduling a time is important to help you get into a regular routine of sitting down with God to spend time with Him, eating the meal He has prepared for you. God has prepared a fresh, wholesome spiritual feast to meet all of our spiritual nutritional needs. Thirty minutes a day spent eating of His feast will make you spiritually strong and healthy, and it's the best way you can possibly complete your day!

Thirty minutes, however, shouldn't be your outer limit. The more time you spend alone at the dinner table with God, the more you will begin to develop good spiritual eating habits. God expects us, as His children, to imitate His Son, Jesus Christ, and good spiritual eating habits will cause us to become wise in Him: we will start to like what Jesus likes, know what He knows, look like He looks, and act like He acts. Our joy will be increased, and our prayers will be answered because we too will know what to pray for according to God's will for our lives.

As you sit down to dine, it will be useful to get a notebook (or use Your Daily Bread Spiritual Journal in this book) to write down everything you learn while sitting at the spiritual dinner table and during your Royal Candlelight Devotional Moments with God in the mornings.

The Temptation to Cancel Your Reservations

The Lord looks forward to your daily dinner reservations for two. Bible study is an opportunity for you to create an atmosphere of worshiping Him in spirit and in truth. It is a good time for you to work on your personal, one-on-one, intimate relationship with God. Scripture tells us that Jesus is standing at the door of our hearts, knocking and waiting for us to let Him in so that He can sit down and dine with us: "Behold, I stand at the door and knock. If anyone hears My voice and opens the door, I will come in to him and dine with him, and he with Me" (Revelation 3:20).

At times, we are all tempted to cancel our dinner reservations— perhaps we're tired, or distracted, or not feeling well. But just think of how disappointing it would be if you were to keep making dinner reservations with someone you loved, only to deal with a continual response of "I can't make it; I have to cancel our reservations again." Imagine knowing that someone you love is continually putting you last on his or her list of things to do. It would be clear that this person does not value your relationship. Eventually, you get the feeling that he or she doesn't really love you, despite words to the contrary.

If we do not know God, we can't possibly feel His broken heart or know the disappointment He feels when we choose not to sit down alone with Him. Well, my brothers and sisters in Christ, I'm here to tell you that we break God's heart every time we put Him last on our list of things to do and cancel our daily reservations because we do not value relationship with Him.

Uninvited Guests

In the beginning, two uninvited guests will always show up to try to destroy your evening. One party crasher you need to be aware of goes by the name of Satan. He is aware of your intentions to keep your dinner date, and he will make every attempt to interrupt you. Satan will try to interrupt you by whispering "sweet nothings" in your ear (just like he did with Eve), deceitful tactics that will cause you to doubt and reject God and His Word. Satan is also good at sending fear to distract you and cause you to worry about whether God's Word is really true because of what you may be going through at the time. At that moment, you must guard your heart. If you let fear enter, faith has less of a chance to operate on your behalf by trusting God's Word, obeying His commandments, or pleasing Him.

Satan's "sweet nothings" sound good at the time, but they are nothing but bitter trouble for you because they are nothing but empty promises that will cause you to turn away from God and keep you from focusing (looking at God), thinking (meditating on His Word), and spending time (building a relationship) with Him. You end up with nothing because you missed out on God's promises, which are found in His Word, and His blessings, the sweet treats you could have enjoyed dining on if you had not been interrupted by the intruder. When he shows up at the door of your heart, don't let him in. Remember, God told us that Satan could show up disguised as an "angel of light" (2 Corinthians 11:14). You need to slam the door in his face by resisting him. He, in turn, will have to flee the premises of your heart (James 4:7).

Your flesh is the other uninvited guest who will begin to start trouble. Your flesh will war against your spirit, trying to stop you from sitting down to eat of God's Word. Your mind will start to fill up with all kinds of distractions. A battle is going on between the spirit and the flesh, each one trying to get its way in order to take control of your actions.

The spirit tells you what's the right thing to do, and the flesh reminds you of everything that *seems* too important to put off until later. Its goal is to take your mind off of God, who should be your top priority, and put it on less important issues that will become a high priority for you if you let them. If you are not careful, the flesh will cause you to put off eating a full meal, settling for a halfhearted snack instead. Remember, God is not of importance to you, unless He becomes supremely important to you. I encourage you stay focused on completing the meal no matter what is going on. Don't just settle for less nourishing fast food!

Eventually, both intruders will stop trying so hard to spoil your time alone with God. They will finally get the message that you have made up your mind to make God your priority, and they will not be allowed to interfere with any more reservations you make with God.

Conversing with the King

When keeping your dinner reservations with the King, you will also have a great opportunity to discuss your personal concerns over dinner. Just like in the meal (book) of Esther, you too can place yourself in a good position to find favor in the King's sight as you drink the Aged Royal Wine at the banquet from the King's banquet table. The King can grant you the petition and do what you have requested of Him (Esther 4:6–8) because you revealed all your needs at the banquet table that the Master Chef prepared. While you are dining with the King, He just might ask *you,* "What is your petition? It shall be granted to you, and what is your request?" (See Esther 7:2).

Chapter 12

Compliments to the Master Chef

"I will bless the LORD at all times;
His praise shall continually be in my mouth.
My soul shall make its boast in the Lord."
—Psalm 34:1–2

Chapter 12
Compliments to the Master Chef

God tells us to greet one another with a holy kiss in Romans 16:16 but have you ever thought about greeting God by *kissing His presence* every morning with prayer and complimenting Him with thanksgiving? Romans 16:16 is about greeting each other and expressing our love, but what about greeting and expressing your love toward God?

A holy kiss to God, first thing every morning, is your way of allowing God to be your very first thought in the day. God is not far from each of us—for in Him we live, move, and exist (Acts 17:27–28). He has provided us with the very breath we breathe every day. That means He is right there when you wake up every morning! When you open your eyes, the first thing you should want to do is to kiss the Lord with prayer and greet Him with thanksgiving.

A kiss is a sign of affection and endearment. It's two people coming together in approval, and it is a sweet way of greeting someone. Kissing God's presence is as easy as saying "Good morning, Lord; I love You." Such prayer is a simple form of thanksgiving and rejoicing in praise to welcome the God of our salvation into our busy day.

Kissing His presence is also a form of worship. We tend to think of *worship* as just kneeling down and reciting praises, singing a song, or shouting loud blessings to God. But the Greek word for worship is *proskuneo,* which translates to *reverence,* meaning "to glory, honor, or praise." It comes from two words: *pro,* which means *toward,* and *kuneo,* which means *kiss – as one would kiss the hand or go towards one, in token of reverence.* What does *worship* mean in Greek? It is *to kiss God,* an allegory that describes our intimate relationship with Him.

In the Song of Solomon 1:2, the very first words are, "Let him smother me with kisses from his mouth, for his love is better than wine" (NASB). God smothers us every day with kisses in His love for us, so in our worship to God, we should kiss Him back. How can we be in a loving relationship without kissing each other? When we worship God, we kiss from the heart because it is the simple, natural, and intimate thing to do. The next time you wake up in the morning, close your eyes and just start kissing God . . . with worship.

There is no rule that says we only have to meet and greet God in the morning. Try having other quiet moments alone with God during your lunch break and at night before you go to bed. Also, practice allowing God's thoughts to run through your mind all during the day. Talking to God all day about everything that concerns you is "praying without ceasing" (1 Thessalonians 5:17). There is no set amount of time you must spend with God, as long as you are consistent in spending time with Him on a daily basis. You can even add singing a song of praise during your quiet time. Bowing down in your heart at the feet of the Lord to serenade Him with a new song every day is another form of exalting and honoring the One you truly adore. Psalm 149:1 tells us to "Praise the Lord! Sing to the Lord a new song."

While we can pray and praise all day long, study requires more focus. Set a time to eat your spiritual dinner when you will be able to concentrate on the meal. There is nothing more important and natural than this. We have been called to have fellowship with God ever since the beginning, when God met with Adam in the Garden of Eden. Christ died on the cross to restore the fellowship with God that was broken when Adam fell into sin. When we stay in touch with God on a daily basis, our fellowship will be a great source of strength for us. It is absolutely essential to our spiritual health to spend quality time alone with our heavenly Father every day.

We know that physically, we cannot possibly live off of just one meal a week. Yet, many of us try it spiritually when our only source of spiritual food is a Sunday sermon. Imagine your starving spiritual body having the same physical appearance as those we see on TV suffering from malnutrition, with their fragile ribs and swollen stomachs, unable to function normally due to their lack of energy and slowly dying for lack of physical food. Just like we need daily food for our physical bodies, our spiritual bodies require daily spiritual food also. Too little spiritual food can create spiritual anemia, malnutrition, and even death. Spiritual food transforms into spiritual energy, and that energy enables us to do what God wants us to do to please Him.

When I was growing up, both my parents worked, so my grandmother had the responsibility of taking care of my cousins and me during the day. I remember coming in every day from playing outside. She would always tell us to go and wash our faces and hands before we sat down at the table to eat. We were taught to say grace ("God is great; God is good; let us thank Him for our food. Amen") before we ate, and we had to eat everything that was put on our plates, without the luxury of complaining about what we did not like to eat! When my grandmother saw us frowning at food we didn't like, she would remind us that we should be grateful to get a hot meal every day, because there were children in other parts of the world who were starving to death and would be glad to get such a meal. My grandmother wanted to teach us at a young age to praise God and be grateful for what she knew God had provided for us. Even though we said this prayer before every meal, our frowning up showed that we really didn't appreciate what we had received, so she had to remind us just how blessed we were by God who is great in everything and very good to us also.

Today, I find that God is telling us the very same thing my grandmother used to tell me, but from a spiritual perspective. Once we make the decision to come into the household of faith after playing out in the dirt of our sinful lives, God tells us to come into His house and wash our faces and hands from all our filthiness. We are to sit down at the dinner table because He has prepared a wholesome meal for us. He expects us to say grace and thank Him for the food we are about to receive, for the nourishment of our bodies for Christ's sake. Some of us need to stop frowning and complaining at God's greatness and goodness that He has placed on our plate to eat and show some appreciation for what the Master Chef has prepared for us, because there are those all over the world still spiritually starving to death.

At times, the meals may not be to our taste, but our heavenly Father knows what is good for us, and we should be grateful. There are those less fortunate than ourselves who are still outside, playing in the dirt of this sinful world without a clue about their filthy, poverty-stricken condition. They are spiritually starving to death, and they don't even know that Christ gave His life to prepare us a feast to dine on at the King's banquet table. Their unfit and abusive spiritual daddy, Satan, cannot provide for them, nor does he care about their spiritual, physical, emotional, social, or financial well-being like Christ does.

Coming into His Presence

In complimenting the Master Chef, Jesus Christ, we should also consider our desire and practice being in His presence. Many Christians desire the promises of God without ever considering what it means to be in the presence of God—they prefer the hand of God to the face of God, wanting to receive something from Him without an actual relationship. As His children, we should always look forward to being in the presence of God, especially while we are studying His Word. This is a time when we can communicate with Him one-on-one; face-to-face, through prayer and meditation on His Word—a time when we can receive the blessing of God as He speaks to us through His Word.

Moses, whom God considered a friend, met face-to-face with God (Exodus 33:11). To be in the presence of God is the most glorious position for a child of God! Moses knew how much more important it was to be in the presence of God than just to have His promises. Being in the presence of God gives us direct access to Him, because as His children, we are free to approach the King at any time, day or night. But we must come for the right reasons, because it's not always about what you can get from God, but it's also about getting to know God for yourself.

There were things that God only shared with Moses, but Moses had to come to the Tent of Meeting so that God could commune with him. When you come to meet with God, there are things God will share with you also because of your relationship and position in Him (Exodus 33:11 and James 2:1). When God decides to commune with you spiritually face-to-face as a friend, you are in the presence of His glory, and that puts you in an amazing and glorious position. In a spiritual sense, your face will shine brightly just like Moses' did each time you meet with God: glowing from the joy and excitement of being with the King and knowing for yourself just how much God loves you.

God's presence is security and assurance for the believer, because where there is light, darkness can't appear—Satan can't get at us in the presence of God! Coming into God's presence gives us the opportunity to enjoy the Father's friendship and fellowship, along with that of His Son and the Holy Spirit. We can experience not only unity and intimacy with the Trinity, but the reception of confidential information as well, because when God considers us friends, He makes Himself known by revealing the awesome and marvelous secrets and mysteries of His excellent greatness. (John 15:15 – "...but I have called you friends for all things that I have heard from My Father I have made known to you.") He plans for us to continue to spend quality time with Him forever. (Acts 2:38 – "Thou hast made known to me the ways of life; Thou wilt make me full of gladness with Thy presence." NASB)

For some of us who prefer the hand of God to the face of God, our avoidance of His presence is because we are not willing to change the way we live, turning from our wicked ways and allowing God to truly be Lord of our lives. Carnality causes our refusal to crown Him King over our lives. We don't want God to see us in our sin. We find ourselves running and hiding from the Lord; covering up our sin with leaves of excuses, but our nakedness is always before the Lord, who sees and knows everything.

If God is not on the throne of your heart, stop putting the blame on someone or something else. I encourage every believer facing this issue to repent by confessing their sins and turning their hearts toward God so they can stand blameless before Him. The fact is, you can't get anything from His hand without His heart! The carnal man needs to get rid of the pride that is harbored inside his heart and humble himself before the Lord (1 Corinthians 2:14 and 3:2). Humility will draw God's attention toward you. You see, you can't get anything from God's heart if He has turned His back to you and His face is not facing you, with the eyes of His favor toward you. I strongly encourage you to repent (turn around) and turn your heart back toward God, because you can't receive anything from God's hand without first touching His heart.

God's presence will bring you perfect peace and rest because of the love that accompanies it. If you are tired of running from God because of your sinful ways, try turning toward Him and showing Him that you have a repentant heart that desires to have Him on its throne, guiding you in all your ways and decisions. You must come into the presence of God with a humble heart and the right mindset that shows God that you want Him alone to be Lord of your life. A mind that is clothed in God's righteousness and goodness will have no need to hide from His presence when He looks for you.

Instructions on how to enter God's presence are found in John 15:4-11, where God tells us to abide in Him and He will abide in us. You must abide in God's love to experience His presence and be considered His friend, and if you do what He commands you to do, the Lord will make His presence known to you by sharing with you what our Father has told Him. The condition is to abide in Christ and let His words abide in you so that you can ask what you wish and it will be done for you (John 15:7).

Enter God's presence with a humble heart and a mind open to the will of God, with the expectation that God will come to commune with you simply because you have come to meet with Him. Don't forget to cultivate a willingness to do whatever God instructs you to do for Him. Be prayerful and grateful to God for allowing you to come into His glorious presence.

God will always keep His promises, but to seek to acquire them without wanting to be in His presence makes us vulnerable to the presence of Satan, our spiritual enemy, whom we can't see, but who sees us and attacks us without invitation. Unlike God, Satan will invade our privacy every chance he gets in order to influence our every thought, feeling, and action so that he can kill, steal from, and destroy us. In his deceptive schemes, he will try to get us to question and reject our Father's plans for our lives. Because we have been adopted and given a new last name as "Christians," Satan has no legal right to control or influence us unless we let him.

Remember, without God we can do absolutely nothing; we cannot even move or have our being (Acts 17:18). When you come into the presence of God, expect to fill your spiritual stomach with wisdom, your head with knowledge, and your heart with understanding. You will always leave His spiritual table with blessings that will give you all the more reason to compliment the Master Chef. Time in His presence will leave you wanting more, because you have delighted in spending time with the Master Chef. You will come away glowing and radiating with joy: you have come spiritually face-to-face with the God of the universe, and He chose to meet you personally!

Your divine Best Friend has not only placed blessings in your hand, feeding you with divine delicacies that will nourish you for eternity, but He will also open your blinded eyes to see His glory. That in itself is reason enough to compliment Him once you see and experience how beautiful God is toward you!

A Personal Recipe From
§ The Spiritual Gourmet Chef's Kitchen §

Are you physically hungry? Then try this appetizer, created by your Spiritual Gourmet Chef:
something to perk up your appetite while you continue to read this devotional cookbook.

Appetizer Recipe

Angel Shrimp & Crab Stuffed Eggs

1 can shrimp
1 can crab meat
6 boiled eggs
¼ cup chopped green onion
¼ cup chopped celery
2 teaspoons Lawry's Season-All
1 teaspoon garlic powder
½ teaspoon mustard
¼ tablespoon sugar
¼ cup Miracle Whip or mayonnaise
1 small can sliced black olives
Paprika

Cut eggs in half lengthwise and remove the yolk from each white half. Mash the yolks and add the ingredients (except for the sliced black olives), and mix to a smooth paste. Fill the egg white halves using a spoon, or you can use a pastry bag with a star tip for a decorative presentation. Garnish the top of each egg with a dash of paprika and a sliced black olive.

Other garnishes to use in decorating the top of each egg:

Chopped Parsley

Capers

Diced Pimiento

Service of 12 Eggs

Heavenly!

Chapter 13

Gaining a Spiritual Appetite

"My eyes are ever toward the LORD."
—Psalm 25:15

Chapter 13
Gaining a Spiritual Appetite

*I*n order for our studies to be profitable, we need to cultivate a love for the Bible as well as a love for Jesus. The Bible is the only answer to our spiritual hunger. The believer who has a real appetite for God's Word will gain more out of it than the believer who only reads God's Word out of necessity. You need to come to the dinner table craving the spiritual meals that have been prepared for you. Studying God's Word on a regular basis will satisfy that craving. It will also increase your appetite and sharpen your cravings as you learn to love the Word!

If you are frustrated, never fear. You also need to develop patience with yourself and allow the Master Chef to reveal His culinary treasures. However, take precautions so you don't behave like a picky eater of God's Word. God doesn't ask us what we want to eat. Instead, He has prepared meals for the nourishment of our spiritual bodies, and He expects us to eat everything that He puts on our plates.

Take time to properly chew your food. Meditate on the Word as you read it. Some spiritual foods will be unfamiliar to you, but don't push them aside or rush through them too quickly. The food may not always taste good at first, but keep trying it—it is good for you, and you will grow to like it. When we were children, many of us disliked vegetables, but many of our parents gave them to us anyway because they knew they were good for us. When we grew up, we learned to love these same foods, and we now give them to our children for the same reasons our parents gave them to us. Well, guess what, saints: our Heavenly Parent knows exactly what is best for us too. He provides us with what we need as opposed to just what we want!

As you dine each day, you will gain knowledge of who God is and of His purpose for your life. You will also learn why the treasures of His Word are hidden from the unbeliever, but not from you, who seek to dig deep into the pot of spiritual food to find the Lamb. We receive power from His Word when we are willing to work hard and be disciplined in seeking Him daily. Studying the Bible requires thinking, so you cannot be intellectually lazy if you want your study to be profitable. Think of the time you waste every day doing things that profit you nothing, when you could be taking the time to study to show yourself approved unto God, able to rightly divide this Word of truth!

When you are well-fed on the Word of God, you will not be ashamed to talk with unbelievers or with people of other faiths. You can stand with faith, share your faith, and be the one God will faithfully use to win someone over to the Faith of Christ because you are capable of sharing the knowledge you have obtained through your dedicated study.

God's home-cooked meals are so good that they will alter your attitude toward other things as well. Your new joy and perspective will show the world the amazing image of God as you become a good witness for Him, sharing your personal testimonies of the goodness of God and the nourishment you gain at the Father's table each day. (Nehemiah 8:18b: There was a great rejoicing, "and he read from the book of the law of God daily, from the first day to the last day. And they celebrated the feast seven days.")

And don't be afraid that God's bounty will run out! Jesus is a Master at converting the raw food material of the Bible into many portions of food for the soul that can and will continue to feed millions, just as He did back when He took two fish and five loaves of bread that physically fed five thousand men, besides women and children, and still had twelve baskets of bread and fish left over (Matthew 14:17–21 and Mark 6: 41–44). God's provision for you will never run out!

Continue to be faithful over a few things so that God can make you ruler over many. Studying God's Word is profitable. Not only that, but it contains an abundance of special after-dinner mints of promises and sweet treats of blessings for His children. As you diligently seek Him, being consistent in your studies of the Bible, you'll be able to find out what God has promised you and what your responsibilities are in order to claim these promises so that you may be continually blessed as you increase your appetite for God's Word.

Chapter 14

Eating at the King's Banquet Table: Fundamental Dining Techniques

"Your words were found and I ate them,
and Your word was to me the joy and rejoicing of my heart."
—Jeremiah 15:16

Chapter 14

Eating at the King's Banquet Table:
Fundamental Dining Etiquette

*J*ust as those who sit down to a royal feast must learn proper etiquette and order, handlers of God's Word must learn to use the proper methods and utensils for dining also.

Routines and Etiquette

In this book and all of its related Bible studies (The Royal Candlelight Culinary Recipe Book Series), you will be instructed to read a selected book of the Bible at one sitting and repeat your reading of the same book five times. This can be considered part of your devotional reading (your Royal Candlelight Moments) where you are just sitting before the Lord to read His Word. This can be done early in the morning, before you start your day, as you rise early to meet and fellowship with Jesus.

To help yourself commit to this daily routine, eat a spiritual meal *before* you eat a physical one. If you routinely skip breakfast, make sure you eat at least a spiritual breakfast bar or snack—a chapter or two on weekdays; five chapters on Sunday—before you physically eat anything at all. This means you may have to get up fifteen or twenty minutes earlier to feed your spiritual body before going about your busy day.

- **Before you start eating, *season your food with prayer*.** Seasoning is one of the most important skills for a seeker of God to develop. In cooking, seasoning enhances the natural flavor of food without significantly changing its original flavor. Prayer does much the same thing for our study time. And saying grace (or giving thanks to God) before every meal is an appropriate practice at the King's table as well as at our physical dinner tables! Before you begin any Bible study, pray for God to enhance your taste buds so that you will be able to "taste and see that the Lord is good" (Psalm 34:8).

You also want to pray to be forgiven, because you don't want to come to the dinner table with a dirty face and hands. Freshen up before you eat: pray to be cleansed of all unrighteousness. You have the privilege of dining with the King, and He can share with you how the Master Chef has prepared each meal. You should want to be in the presence of God to make your fellowship time meaningful and joyful as you come together in love.

While you are at the dinner table, spend some time meditating, or prayerfully thinking and concentrating, on the meal. Ask the Master Chef to show you how to live out His instructions and wisdom to make you a pleasing sight to Him and to give Him glory.

- **Take your personally prescribed spiritual vitamins and supplements of praise and worship.** The vitamins and supplements of praise and worship are important to nutrition and body function. Spend a moment telling the Master Chef how much you appreciate these divinely prepared meals, skillfully blended just for you with the exquisite spices of love and sweet herbs of compassion. It will be most pleasing to the Lord if you take time to praise and worship Him, and you will notice an effect on the spiritual food you are about to eat—and on your spiritual life all through the day, especially when you compliment the Master Chef.

- **Don't forget to ask God for the Aged Royal Wine, which compliments each meal and will help you digest your food.** We suggest you drink a *full glass each time you dine.* The Holy Spirit is the One who teaches us everything we need to know about the Word of God. The Aged Royal Wine is full of the natural proteins of love, joy, peace, patience, kindness, goodness, faithfulness, gentleness, and self-control. These Fruit of the Spirit ingredients sweeten the taste of the knowledge of Christ Jesus. *There are no added preservatives or passion fruits of desire and immorality mixed into this drink* (see Galatians 5:22).

  The Aged Royal Wine comes with a seal of approval directly from the Master Chef that guarantees your safety against food-borne illnesses: Ephesians 1:14 tells us that the Holy Spirit is the guarantee of our inheritance until the redemption of the purchased possession, to the praise of His glory. Being filled with the Holy Spirit does not leave any room for unwanted spiritual bacteria or parasites to contaminate your spiritual body.

- **When dining from the dinner table, don't leave any food on your plate.** When possible, read the book you have selected at one sitting. This will help you grasp a general knowledge of what you will be studying, and again, this can be done during your devotional time with God. There is an abundance of food to feed on at the King's banquet table, so feast on as much as you can now. There will be much more for you to dine on tomorrow. In instances when the books of the Bible are too long to read at one sitting, decide on what chapters you are going to read each day until you complete the book. Like Scripture says in 2 Kings 4:43, "Give them to people that they may eat for thus says the Lord, They shall eat and have some left over" (NASB).

- **Repeat the reading of the book five times.** You want to familiarize yourself with the unforgettable, savory flavors you will taste before you begin to gain understanding. Reading a book repeatedly enables you to taste, see, and feel the flow of the book. Reading it in different translations will give you additional insights as you view each translator's rendering of the original writing. Take notes on the interesting differences you discover from each translation.

- **While you are dining with the King, write down what the Master Chef reveals to you during your conversation.** *Take time in chewing your food (meditating) so that you can enjoy every bite.* This is a good time to get to know the Lord and develop an intimate relationship by asking questions about the irresistible recipes you are feasting on. Meditating is taking the necessary time to think and process what you have read, allowing the truth to marinate and preparing you to apply what you have learned so you can readjust every area of your life where necessary. Joshua 1:8 and Psalm 1:1–2 tell us to meditate on the Word of God day and night. Meditation is a time when we can ask ourselves if there is some part of our lives where the truth is needed so we can do according to all that is written in the Word, to delight in the law of the Lord and to make our way prosperous so we will have good success.

- **Be sure to enjoy a salad with your entrée.** Pick "salads" of verses that can be *memorized* to go along with the "entrées" of chapters and books. The best verse to memorize is the main verse of the chapter you are studying. Study and take note of all the ingredients in each memory verse you choose. The texture of the vegetables and fruit may be raw so that you have to spend some time chewing on them, or they may be cooked for tenderness so they are quicker or easier to swallow (understand).

- **Use proper eating utensils.** Of course, we all know that it is not proper etiquette to eat a meal without using the proper utensils! Use the "silverware" resources listed below to assist you in studying Scripture so that you will not miss a single bite.

- *A Sharp Knife (Good Study Bible).* Hebrews 4:12 mentions that God's Word is like a two-edged sword. Consistent use of a good study Bible helps us become skillful in the Word, helping us to properly slice the meat of the Word without cutting ourselves by misquoting Scripture or taking it out of its context. It is the foremost utensil to use in becoming a great connoisseur of spiritual foods. Look for a study Bible complete with both Old and New Testaments, with a concordance in the back. I have found *The New American Standard Hebrew-Greek Key Study Bible* very easy to read and very helpful in studying God's Word. It contains a concordance, a lexicon aid to the Old and New Testaments, grammatical notations, and *Strong's Hebrew and Greek Dictionary*.

- *A **Dinner Fork** (Concordance).* This utensil is used for picking up selected portions of food for meditation and understanding. A concordance is great when you want to know the meaning of a word used in a particular text.

- *A **Salad Fork** (Bible Dictionary or Bible Encyclopedia).* This utensil can be used to pick up subjects, words, places, and doctrines for fully described, accurate meanings. This utensil is extremely valuable for word and term study because it explains meaning in context. It also includes illustrations, genealogical tables, maps, and other information that will spread a dressing of life into the text.

- *A **Dinner Spoon** (Commentary).* Just like in physical dining, this utensil is one that you may not need to use that often. If you do, be careful when using it for stirring, mixing, and serving any ingredients in the meal that might act as lumps of misunderstanding. There are a large number of commentaries to choose from, but I personally prefer to use *Matthew Henry's Commentary*. Although commentaries are useful, I must warn you not to strictly rely on this secondhand knowledge. Again, it is the juices from someone else's taste buds, and you want to "fine dine" on God's Word yourself first before relying on other resources. God would have you to first taste the flavors of His Word for yourself.

- *A Dessert Fork (Handbook)*. This utensil is helpful in picking up sweet biblical information about every book in the Bible. It can give irresistible facts and fascinating tidbits about archeological findings during the four hundred years of God's silence between the Old and New Testaments. This utensil will also give some additional background knowledge, which adds a special treat to your study for clarity and understanding of the culture and what took place during that time in history. I recommend *Halley's Handbook* because it contains biblical and historical facts that a Christian might find very helpful and useful. It also includes an abbreviated Bible commentary and archaeological discoveries that further prove that what we believe is the truth. It also tells how we got our Bible and summarizes fascinating features of church history. You will find it has some awesome photographic illustrations and it outlines the Bible story for you as well.

Note: If you don't have all of these eating utensils in your spiritual kitchen, they can be found in your local shopping areas as you search though the aisles of the internet *(the following websites)*:

- www.studylight.org
- www.blueletterbible.org
- www.bible.org

A Personal Recipe From
§ The Spiritual Gourmet Chef's Kitchen §

Have you been faithful in your study of God's Word?
Then try this recipe created by your Spiritual Gourmet Chef.
Go and wash your face and hands; say grace to thank God for the
food you are about to eat.
Then sit down and dine on this hot meal
to nourish your physical body.

Soup Recipe

Faithful Seafood Soup

¼ cup chopped green onion
¼ cup chopped green pepper
¼ cup chopped celery
2 tablespoons butter
Two 13 oz. cans of chicken broth
¼ pound fresh crab meat
¼ pound fresh shrimp (peeled)
One 6 oz. can minced or fresh clams
¼ cup fresh broccoli tops
1 can baby corn, whole
¼ cup of baby carrots
¼ cup of pea pods
¼ teaspoon Lawry's Season-All
1 tablespoon parsley
¼ teaspoon garlic powder
1 package Lipton Onion Soup Mix
2 teaspoons ground shrimp (seasoning)
½ teaspoon Old Bay seasoning

In a large saucepan, sauté onion, green pepper, and celery in butter until tender. Add the shrimp, crab meat, and clams to mixture. Mix Lipton Onion Soup Mix with chicken broth and add to saucepan. Let simmer for 10 minutes. Add broccoli tops, baby corn, baby carrots, pea pods, and seasoning to saucepan. Cover and let simmer for 30 minutes. Pour over steamed rice or noodles.

This soup goes well with your favorite brand of crackers.

Trustworthy!

Chapter 15

Mise en Place

*"Therefore take up the whole armor of God,
that you may be able to withstand in the evil day,
and having done all, to stand."*
—Ephesians 6:13

Chapter 15
Mise en Place

Mise en place is a French term used in culinary circles: it means *preparation.* In today's commercial kitchens, it is called *prepping* or *prep work.* Prep work is simply making sure you have everything in place, that you are not missing anything required to complete your meal. In other words, all preparation and organization must be made before the actual production begins.

In Bible study, preparation is just as important. You are going to be required to prep your mind, body, and heart to receive what the Master Chef will serve. You also want to make sure you have your personally prescribed vitamins and supplements (praise and worship), seasoning for your food (prayer), a full glass of the Aged Royal Wine (the Holy Spirit), and your eating utensils (resource materials). These all need to be brought to the dinner table, along with your menu selection (selected Scripture to study) for the day.

Preparation of the Mind

To prepare your mind, you must train it to put God first in all things so you won't fall prey to the desires of Satan and your sinful flesh. Make the necessary adjustments to keep your daily dinner reservation with the King, and come to the dinner table expecting to sit down in the presence of God and experience the delight of dining with the very *Bread of Life* Himself, anticipating that a new and exciting mystery of God will be revealed to you while you are at the spiritual dinner table.

Staying Focus When You're Not Excited

There may be times when studying is not as exciting and new, but don't allow your mind to play tricks on you by telling yourself that, for example, you've already read this Scripture so you don't need to read it again. That's when you start to think that you "know it all"—when you don't. No matter how many times you read the Bible, you will discover something exciting and new that you missed the last time you read this particular Scripture. I encourage you to keep seeking. When God sees your desire to continue regardless of how you feel, then He can decide to open your eyes and reveal more of His mysteries and let you taste the ingredients He put in that meal so that you can discover something exciting and new about Him.

Remember to always pray before reading God's Word. Ask Him to reveal Himself to you, and then rely on the Holy Spirit to guide and teach you in that which you missed the last time. You can never learn everything you need to know to apply to your life all at one time…it's a growing process and a journey God wants you to take on with Him. Ask Him to bless you with an excitement and a love for His Word because you want to be pleasing to Him, because you want Him to look at you with the excitement and delight He has in His heart for you, all because you are delighted in reading His Word. God has also promised to give you the desires of your heart if you delight in Him (Psalm 37:4). Even when you are tired or can't muster up your own excitement, you can see that there are benefits to studying.

Opening up God's Word is like looking into the face of God. *Reading* His Word allows you to gaze into the eyes of God as He speaks to you from His heart about His love for you. When you learn about God, it is as if you are laying your head against His chest to hear and feel His heart beating just for you. God has poured His love into His Word so you will know how to find Him when you seek Him with your whole heart (Deuteronomy 4:29).

Preparation of the Body

Physical preparation is also necessary for enjoying a good spiritual dinner. Physically position yourself so that you will not get too relaxed. You want to be in a place where you can concentrate fully on your meal, without any interruptions or disturbances. Your posture should be upright, not lying down. You don't want to get sleepy! Again, your flesh is going to do its part to get you to stop what you are doing by telling you that you are too tired and sleepy to finish your meal. (In most cases, you will notice that the minute you decide to discontinue studying, the sleepiness will immediately vanish.)

Allow the Spirit to take control to convince you that you need to continue eating. At the dinner table with God, the flesh should not have victory over the spirit.

Preparation of the Heart

As you sit down to dine, focus your attitude and motives, opening your heart to the Spirit of God as He teaches you the mysteries of who He is and who you are in Christ. The aromas of His Word will begin to fill your heart, and its flavors will be sweet and pleasurable to your taste.

However, we cannot address preparation of the heart without recognizing, based on Matthew 15:19 that from the heart comes evil thoughts, murders, adultery, fornications, thefts, lying, and slander. Ask God to give you a clean heart. Confess the sin in your heart, like King David did when he invited God to change His heart condition in Psalm 51:10: "Create in me a clean heart, O God, and renew a steadfast spirit within me."

Don't Give In, Don't Give Up, and Don't Give Out

Don't give in to the pressures of Satan and your flesh as they try to take charge of your actions. Don't give up on the pursuit of precious minutes with God. Don't give out on learning for yourself what it takes to know God and make healthy spiritual eating choices.

These preparations allow you to taste what has been cooking all these years in the magnificent royal meals of the Master Chef, Jesus. You will experience the nourishment and incredible taste of the Word of God coming together and will be able to appreciate, from the heart, the great sacrifice it took for the Master Chef to present it to you.

A Thirty-Minute Meal

All this prepping should take place before your Royal Dinner is served each day. Once prep work is complete, you are ready to sit down to a great dining experience that should last at least thirty minutes.

Just about everybody these days wants to eat fast food, but what we are finding out in the culinary world is that it really isn't good to always dine on fast food. These foods often lack the nutritional value required to meet our nutritional needs. We, as Christians, find ourselves desiring God's Word in the same quick-and-easy manner. Some of us want to eat and run because we are too busy to sit down and dine on spiritually wholesome, nutritious, home-cooked food. We lack spiritual nutrients, and so we are not living life abundantly. We fail to understand what causes our frustrations, so we drive up to the "Windows of Heaven," wanting God to open those windows and hand out blessings after taking our order.

God has already told us in His Word that He is standing at the door of our hearts, knocking and waiting for us to let Him in so that

He can come in and sit down to dine with us (Revelation 3:20). He will deal with all of our issues while reclining at the dinner table, but we must take the time to show up, sit down, and truly feast. (Luke 14:17 "And at the dinner hour he sent his slave to say to those who had been invited, come; for everything is ready now." And Luke 14:15 "...and when one of those who were *reclining at the table* with Him heard this, he said to Him, blessed is everyone who shall eat bread in the kingdom of God!" NASB)

A Personal Recipe From
§ The Spiritual Gourmet Chef's Kitchen §

Are you enjoying this Spiritual Recipe Book so far?
Then try this next recipe to bring some physical enjoyment
to your palate.
Created by your Spiritual Gourmet Chef to put a smile on your face.

Salad Recipe

Joyful Broccoli & Raisin Salad

2 bunches broccoli (tops only—no stems)
½ cup chopped purple onion
¼ cup raisins
2 cups of Miracle Whip or mayonnaise
2 tablespoons sugar
¼ teaspoon Lawry's Season-All
¼ teaspoon garlic powder

Wash the broccoli tops and let dry. In a large bowl, mix the Miracle Whip or mayonnaise, sugar, purple onion, and seasoning together in a bowl to make a dressing. Add the broccoli and raisins and continue to mix until the broccoli and raisins are uniformly covered with the dressing. Let it chill in the refrigerator until time to serve.

§ The Presentation §
After the salad is plated, you may add garnishes:
Tomato Wedges
Cherry, Grape, or Raisin Tomatoes
Cucumber Slices
Radishes

Pecans or Walnuts
Croutons
Pepper Rings
Hard-Boiled Egg Wedges or Slices

Delightfully Delicious!

Chapter 16

The Menu

*"He brought me to the banqueting house
and his banner over me was love."*
—Song of Solomon 2:4

Chapter 16
The Menu

God's Word offers you a rich feast. Although sometimes your dining experience will be simple and light, at other times, eating of the Word of God is more like a full, multicourse meal. In this chapter, you'll find an overview of the elements you'll face each time you sit down to study the Word.

The Royal Family's Secret Ingredient

In the cooking world, many families will allow you to dine on meals with secret ingredients that have been passed down from generation to generation. These secrets are not shared with anyone outside of the family. The same is true of the secret ingredients in God's Word. It is all right to let unbelievers know about the cuisine, through witnessing and evangelizing, but a person has to be *in* the royal family of God to really know and enjoy the secret ingredients of the Word of God that have been passed down from generation to generation (Genesis to Revelation) and have the privilege of dining on them. Unbelievers will not appreciate or be able to enjoy these meals properly, because they are only prepared for the King's kids. Unless a person is willing to be adopted into God's holy family, he or she will never obtain the right to dine sufficiently. "But the natural man does not receive the things of the Spirit of God, for they are foolishness to him; nor can he know them, because they are spiritually discerned" (1 Corinthians 2:14).

So what is the chief secret ingredient in the Word of God? Elsewhere, we've called the main ingredient of God's Word "Lamb." Our Lord and Savior Himself is the Royal Family's Main

Secret Ingredient! He is present in every book of the Bible for us to taste and see His goodness. He may not be obvious, but you will find Him if you seek Him when you dig deep into studying His Word.

A Cup of Soup for Salvation

This dish is not one of the courses offered on the banquet table in the house of God. The Cup of Soup is offered to those outside of God's house and is actually prepared by the Master Chef for the spiritually poor, lost, and poverty-stricken to dine on. The "Soup" for salvation is warm and inviting, and if the lost sinner decides to accept the Soup to feast on, he or she will never have to dine on a cup of soup again. So to all of God's children, who question whether or not they can lose their salvation, get out of the soup line! Once you have accepted the Master Chef's specially prepared dish to save you, you are considered apart of the King's royal family, and you must now dine on the courses of meals offered at the King's banquet table. You are no longer considered poor, but as the King's child, you are one of the princes or princesses who are rich and royal due to your inheritance as one of God's children. Your duty now is to help serve the "Cup of Soup for Salvation" for eternal life (found in John 3:16) to other lost souls in need of a Savior who sit outside of God's royal kingdom.

A Bowl of Stew for Damnation

This is another dish that you won't find at the banquet table in the house of God: STEW (Souls Tasting Eternal Wrath). Back in the day, stew was a meal generally made from leftovers. The only thing the Master Chef has left over to deal with in His universal kitchen is His anger, wrath, and the rejection that was given to Him by all those who hated Him and did not want to love. They chose to deal with God from the back doors of their hearts because they had turned their backs on God.

Studying the Word of God Bite by Bite

In the sections below, you'll find a breakdown of Bible study in culinary terms. The analogies aren't exact—in physical meals, of course, we don't tackle entrées before appetizers—but they may help you remember and categorize the different types of study you want to do. It is a special treat (blessing) when you feast from the King's banquet table (Proverbs 2:10: "When wisdom enters your heart and knowledge is pleasant to your soul . . .").

The Meals

The "meals" are the sixty-six books of the Bible, which hold all the specially prepared delicacies on the King's banquet table that are offered by the Master Chef to the King's children to feast on. When studying the Bible by books, since your spiritual meals start out being only thirty minutes long, you need to start off by choosing a spiritual meal (book) that is short. I recommend beginning with the books of the Bible that contain only one to six chapters and can be read in their entirety at one sitting.

To become entirely familiar with the aromas and flavors of the meal, you should read the same book at least five times before you start dining (studying the book) in earnest. As you get into dining on larger meals with more chapters, you will need to dine on a few selected entrées (chapters) over a longer period until you complete your meal.

The Ingredients

A list of "ingredients," in Bible study terms, is a list of a book's main themes. Listing these and keeping them in mind will help you stay focused as you read, and you'll be able to see the context of individual verses more clearly. Don't forget to search for the Main Secret Ingredient, the Lamb of God, as you focus on the other ingredients in each meal.

The Recipe

The "recipe" is a written summary of the book you are studying. Summaries assist us in gaining a general understanding of the themes and context of a book before we begin to analyze it. In some Bible editions you will find the summary written at the beginning of each book in the Bible. In my Royal Candlelight Culinary Series, which covers all sixty-six books of the Bible, I also provide you with "recipes" in my book-by-book study guides.

The Entrées (Chapter Study)

Enjoying your "entrées" is an allegorical way of picturing the study of the Bible by chapters. You should write an outline for every chapter. Outlining each chapter helps you to discover the main points that will give clarity in what God is pointing out for you so that you may gain knowledge and understanding. Every chapter should yield at least one Great Truth for you to discover.

Chapter study, also called *chapter analysis,* is the process of reading and analyzing each chapter of the book you are studying. Chapter study imparts a delicious knowledge of the meal as a whole.

To gain thorough understanding of a chapter, you will need to examine each paragraph, each verse, and the particular words used. Studying your entrée in such a systematic, careful way enables you to receive knowledge of the Bible in the way it was intended and not in the way you think it should be.

- Use the Chapter Study Form (listed under Study Forms) to complete your chapter study.
- Use the "Outlining the Principal Features of the Meal" Form and Your Daily Bread Spiritual Journal (listed under Forms) to complete your outline.

In the chapters, you will find your "appetizers" (words and terms to study). These are words and terms that are either repeated or strongly emphasized within the text.

The Appetizers (Word & Term Study)

As you read through a chapter, record the "appetizers"—specific words and terms—that jump out as significant. Studying the Bible by words and terms will help you gain meaningful insight into what Scripture is saying to you as opposed to what you want it to say or what you think it might be saying. Word and term study is about finding out what is meant by the words used. Correctly interpreting the Bible depends on having a correct understanding of the words.

At times, you'll be required to use your *Dinner Fork* and *Salad Fork* (concordance and Bible dictionary) to determine how words are used in the context of a passage you are reading. Some words have a slightly different application in different passages of Scripture, or they may have different nuances based on different situations and contexts. The most important factor is to determine the true meaning of a word so that you can fully understand how it is used in its context. Write down what the original word means by using a concordance to find out how a word is used in a particular Scripture. Using cross-references (that is, looking up other Scriptures that use the same words or terms) will give you additional insight.

Oftentimes, certain words are repeated in Scripture. These are key words that are important to consider in studying. When God repeats Himself, it's not because He has forgotten what He said to us; it is because He is making an important point, and we need to take notice! Other words are also significant: even though they are not repeated, they may be strongly emphasized. Pay attention!

- Use the Word and Term Study Form (listed under Study Forms) to complete your word and term study.

The Salads (Verse Study)

As in a fine-dining restaurant, you will get a choice of "salads," which are verses to go with your entrée. In our analogy, "house salads" are the key verses that help you unlock the meaning of a chapter and/or apply it to your life.

Some reference Bibles or study guides will offer a specially prepared "house salad"—an already-marked key verse, sometimes noted with a "key" symbol. I like to refer to the house salad as your main salad because it is the key to what makes the selected entrée so special. If your study Bible has not already identified a main verse, it is necessary for you to do so to help you summarize the chapter you are studying.

Besides the main verse, I also suggest that you choose a verse that speaks to you personally and put that verse to memory. This could be a verse that God wants you to apply to your life or something that speaks into a personal situation you face. This verse will come in handy when God gives you an opportunity to use it in a specific situation or during difficult times when you need to encourage either yourself or someone else.

If possible, pick a verse from each chapter and put it to memory. Write the verse on an index card, then *"Pack a Lunch"* or get an index box to put your cards in. Keep them where you can pull them out and refer to them while dining on your physical lunch and review whenever possible. "Your word I have hidden in my heart, that I might not sin against You" (Psalm 119:11). This is one way of allowing God to personally speak to you through His Word when you desperately need to hear from Him while under attack or being tempted to sin against God.

- Use the Verse-To-Verse Study Form (listed under Study Forms) to complete your verse study.

The Desserts (Character Study)

The characters in Scripture give us another area of study. I've chosen to compare them to "desserts": some are fat-free treats you won't want to skip; others are full of calories that are not good for you. Either way, you need to know what is in them! Some of the people in the Scriptures had good qualities you would do well to emulate; others had lives full of sin and disobedience to God. You want to take notice of them as well, to make sure *your* characteristics don't match up with theirs! God dealt harshly with many of these people because of their sin and disobedience to Him.

Separating the character "desserts" by their ingredients and fat content will help in your knowledge of what is good and what is bad when you prepare your Healthy Dietary and Weight-Loss Programs (more about these later).

As you study a book of the Bible, you can compile a character study by listing the most important people in the book you are studying. Then jot down observations about them. Ask yourself, who are the main people in the book? What do I notice about them? You want to know why they are mentioned, why they are described the way they are, and what is so significant about them that the Master Chef, Jesus Christ, felt it was important to include them as part of

His meals for you. Consider who they are, what they do, and the consequences of their actions, whether positive or negative. Observe their strengths, weaknesses, shortcomings, and outstanding qualities. Remember, the secret ingredient in all of this is Christ Jesus. Character study will give insight into how you can conform to the standards of God and become more Christlike. Write your observations down to help prepare your dietary (life application) and weight-loss (sin-loss) programs.

Suggestion: When studying the characters of Scripture, it is always good to find out if their names have meaning. The meaning of names will further assist you in understanding why these people are included in the Bible and will often offer some clarification to the text when their names show up.

Identify and list the qualities of the characters (positive and negative) by asking yourself questions:

1. What are their characteristics?
2. What causes these characteristics?
3. What are the results of these characteristics?
4. What is the cure (if necessary) for these characteristics?

Note: Be careful not to confuse people who have the same name. For example, one *James* in the Bible is the brother of Jesus; another is a disciple and the son of Zebedee; and another is the son of Alphaeus. Always make sure when studying characters with the same name that you don't get them mixed up!

- Use the Character Study Form (listed under Study Forms) to complete your character study.

The Chief Characters: Father, Son, and Holy Spirit
While dining, notice what name(s) the Trinity uses to describe

Themselves and look out for statements that tell you something about God our Father, Jesus Christ our Lord, or the Holy Spirit our Teacher. Take note of any explanations of the attributes of the Trinity, such as a description of their love, compassion, holiness, justice, grace, mercy, power, patience, lovingkindness, strength, authority, hand (control), faithfulness, anger, and wrath. This will give you the knowledge of who They are and an understanding of Their attributes and characteristics. To top it off, you will learn to fear God, which is the beginning of wisdom, because you will have firsthand knowledge and an understanding of who God the Father, God the Son, and God the Holy Spirit are as One, and you will discover the almighty power and authority they possess according to Proverbs 1:7: "The fear of the Lord is the beginning of knowledge."

Note: You will find that God's lovingkindness is the special dessert topping on every sweet dessert of the Bible's chief characters. It is God's lovingkindness that provides us with after-dinner mints of promises and sweet treats of blessings to end every meal.

After-Dinner Mints and Sweet Treats (God's Promises and Blessings)

The promises God gives us are like the after-dinner mints we receive from upscale restaurants, sealed in wrappers with the restaurant's name imprinted on them as their way of saying, "Thank you for dining with us." God has given us after-dinner mints with His name printed on them which we receive after our obedience to His Word. There are also other *sweet treats,* specially wrapped for us, that we receive from God just by being with Him when He wants to show His love, and they come in the form of blessings. When we study God's Word, we receive God's promises and the blessings of His presence.

- Use Your Daily Bread Spiritual Journal (listed under Study Forms) to record all the sweet and wonderful treats you discover in God's Word—the promises and blessings that are so special to you that you need to write them down to refer back to when you need to be reminded of how great God's goodness tastes to you.

God's spiritual appetizers, salads, entrées, desserts, after-dinner mints, and sweet treats are neatly packaged up as a "square meal" in the pages of the Bible for you to take home to dine on in the privacy of your home, but they can be eaten out in public settings, such as Bible classroom studies. Please don't forget to serve the "Soup" to the unsaved every chance you get, because the King so loves to offer the Master Chef to whosoever is willing to receive Him as their personal Chef: our Lord and Savior, Jesus Christ (John 3:16).

SAMPLE STUDY

In my Royal Candlelight Culinary Series you will find that all sixty-six books of the Bible have been designed as four-course meals for you to dine on once you learn how to properly eat from the King's banquet table. You will really enjoy discovering the great and exciting mysteries of God's Word as you fill up on His spiritual meals to grow healthy and strong in the Lord.

Here is a spiritual meal taken from the book of 1 John, which you will find in one of my follow-up books called Dining By Royal Candlelight.

You can spiritually sample it for yourself. Use the study forms in chapter 22 to complete your meal.

The Meal: 1 JOHN

Sous Chef: *John*   **Date Meal Prepared:** *AD 85–95*

Menu Introduction

The Royal Family Secret Ingredient: Jesus Is Our Advocate

Your meal for today speaks of Christians having fellowship with Christ, who is God incarnate. When Christians walk in the light and are living in love, the result is that they are secure in the eternal life that Christ has given them.

Those who are truly Christ's cannot be eternally lost. Even though they may fall into sin from time to time, this does not affect their position as sons or their eternal salvation, because Christ's death has provided forgiveness for our sins.

Side Dishes of Instructions

1. Season your food with prayer, and take your spiritual vitamins and supplements of praise and worship before you begin your study.

2. If necessary, review the "Spiritual Fundamental Dining Etiquette" found in chapter 14 for further instruction.

3. Pick *one or two salads of verses* that you can put to memory to go along with the five *chapter entrées* you're going to dine on. The "house salad," or main verse, is listed below for you to consider. Study all the ingredients in each salad you choose.

Entrées (Chapter Study)

There are five entrées of chapters to enjoy while dining on this meal. To gain a thorough understanding of each chapter, you will need to read and examine each paragraph, each verse, and the particular words used.

- Chapter 1 – Introduction/The Incarnate Word
- Chapter 2 – Christ Is Our Advocate
- Chapter 3 – Children of God Love One Another
- Chapter 4 – Testing the Spirits
- Chapter 5 – Overcoming the World

Appetizers (Word and Term Study)

Your list of appetizers is generated by using a study Bible that uses a numbered note or symbol to indicate that a particular word or term needs to be clarified by going to the concordance or Bible dictionary. In my Royal Candlelight Culinary Series I have prepared the appetizers menu for each book of the Bible for you; but I have left it up to you to dine on them by looking up the selections to see what they mean. This gives you the opportunity to dine on the knowledge firsthand and gain an understanding for yourself.

Your appetizers of words and terms come out of the entrées of chapters to give you a better understanding of the chapter as a whole.

To study this portion, use your *Dinner Fork* and *Salad Fork* (concordance and Bible dictionary) to find out how these words are used in their scriptural context:

- Advocate
- Fellowship
- Love
- Propitiation
- Walking (in the Light)
- Righteousness
- Incarnation
- Antichrist
- False Prophets
- Born of God

Salads (Verse Study)

Suggested House Salad: 1 John 5:13: "These things I have written to you who believe in the name of the Son of God, that you may know that you have eternal life, and that you may continue to believe in the name of the Son of God."

Recipe for 1 John

Ingredients (Themes): The Incarnation of Christ; Walking in the Light; Living in Love; the Assurance of Salvation.

Recipe (Summary)

The book of 1 John was written to deal with false doctrines. The teachings were to be applied in a congregational setting. The book teaches us that we should pursue the highest moral integrity by striving for a standard of sinless perfection. However, in order to do this, we need to change our eating habits and go on a weight-loss program! Sin in your life can heavily weigh you down. Sinful obesity is very offensive to God and can be very destructive to your spiritual body. It can also destroy those around you. No one obtains instant health, but over a period of time and a good, healthy dietary (life application) program, which includes taking daily supplemental vitamins of prayer, praise, and worship, one can achieve great results just by working on perfecting his or her temple.

John examines the question of whether or not a person who is born of God can commit sin. The one who deliberately, habitually practices sin is of the devil. No one who is born of God practices sin in this way. We cannot easily, maliciously, or deliberately continue to sin, because we are born of God. However, it is possible for a Christian to commit an (uncharacteristic) act of sin. If a Christian sins, he or she has an *Advocate* with the heavenly Father, who is Jesus Christ, the Righteous One.

John was an eyewitness, and he knew that Jesus Christ was not a figment of his imagination, a vision or a dream, but a real person in human form, an authentic manifestation of God in the flesh; and he knew that the genuine knowledge of God will result in the moral transformation of the believer. John saw Jesus in His life and ministry, His transfiguration on the mount, His death on the cross, His return from the grave, and His resurrection from the dead. John wanted to share this testimony and his feeling of joy concerning all he had witnessed, and he wanted to fellowship in Christ and in the Father with all of us in love.

Desserts (Character Study)

There are a variety of "desserts" displayed in this meal to give you a taste of what is good or not good to digest into your own character as you seek to reflect the sweet image and likeness of our personal Master Chef, Jesus Christ. Two desserts have been selected for you to dine on as a sample to see if they are sweet or bitter to your taste buds.

- Jesus Christ *(Advocate)*
- Devil *(Evil One)*

After-Dinner Mints and Sweet Treats (God's Promises and Blessings)

These specially wrapped items, "after-dinner mints" of promises and "sweet treats" of blessings, are the King's and Master Chef's way of saying "thank you" for dining with them because you have met the conditions that were required to receive them. They are placed in God's Word for you to discover as you read, but here is a sample of the promises and blessings found in the book of 1 John:

- Fellowship with the Father and His Son, Jesus Christ.
- Christ forgives us and cleanses us from our sins.
- The promise of eternal life.

I'm sure there are more promises and blessings to discover in this meal, but they are only sweet to you when you dine on them yourself. Continue to search for the promises and blessings as you dine.

Questions

Since you have now dined sufficiently on this book of the Bible, explain what you have digested by answering the following questions from your meal lesson. (These meal lessons are included in each book in my follow-up Royal Candlelight Culinary Series.)

1. Did the Sous Chef John mention any sin that will upset your spiritual stomach and which you need to avoid?
2. Were there any warnings mentioned in this meal?
3. Are there any commands you must follow?
4. What did God tell you about Himself?
5. Explain the difference between committing an act of sin and practicing sin.
6. What were some of the contrasts between walking in the light and walking in darkness?
7. What changes do you need to make concerning your diet that will improve your spiritual body and that you can add to your Healthy Dietary Program?

What Do You Know?

Know is one of the key words repeated in this epistle. First John mentions several things YOU SHOULD KNOW that will assure your eternal life with Christ Jesus.

- List the things you *should* know.
- Design your own Weight-Loss Program, based on what sin you need to lose or avoid.
- Design your Healthy Dietary Program to enhance your character.

Compliments to the Master Chef

Now that you have dined on God's delicious meal, it's proper etiquette for you to respond to such a great meal by complimenting the Master Chef. It will be your way of praising God for what you have received from His Word. Look for every opportunity in His

Word to give Him praise. Here are a few compliments I found when I dined on 1 John, as I sang to God a new song of praise that I had never sung before now:

- Praise God for eternal life *(1:2)*
- Praise God for fellowshipping with us *(1:3)*
- Praise God for the forgiveness of sins *(1:9)*
- Praise God that He has given us an Advocate *(2:1)*
- Praise God for considering us His children *(3:2)*
- Praise God that His commandments are not burdensome *(5:3)*

Personal Recipe From
§ The Spiritual Gourmet Chef's Kitchen §

Now that you have dined on a spiritual meal, here is a special recipe created by your Spiritual Gourmet Chef to feed your physical body.

Entrée Recipe
Soulful Italian Spaghetti Casserole

1 lb. ground beef (substitute ground turkey if you wish)

1 pkg. Lipton Onion Soup Mix

2 large cans tomato sauce

1 pkg. (1lb.) spaghetti

½ cup finely chopped onion

¼ cup largely chopped celery

¼ cup of chopped green pepper

¼ pound Italian sausage

2 cups of grated mild cheddar cheese

1 can stewed tomatoes

2 cloves garlic, crushed

1 teaspoon Lawry's Season-All

2 tablespoon chopped parsley

Oregano

2 tablespoon sugar

Dash of pepper

Olive oil

Scallions (sliced green onions)

Fill a large pot with water. Bring water to a boil. Add spaghetti and a couple of drops of olive oil to keep the spaghetti from sticking together as it boils. (You can also add some seasoning to the boiling water, which adds flavor to the spaghetti while boiling.)

After spaghetti is tender, drain in a colander.

In a separate saucepan, thoroughly brown the ground beef (or ground turkey), and in a pot, boil your Italian sausage. The Italian sausage should then be sliced and added to the ground beef.

In a saucepan, heat a tablespoon of olive oil over a moderate heat. Add onion, celery, green peppers, and garlic; Sauté for 2 minutes or until tender. Mix in tomato sauce, stewed tomatoes, Lipton Onion Soup Mix, and seasoning. Let simmer under low heat for approximately 5 to 7 minutes.

Preheat oven to 350°.

In a casserole dish, add ground beef, Italian sausage, spaghetti, and sauce. Top with grated cheddar cheese and scallions. Place in the oven to heat for 15 minutes.

Spirit-Filled!

Chapter 17

Describing Your Dining Experience

"And the Lord of hosts, will prepare a lavish banquet for all people . . . A banquet of aged wine, choice pieces with marrow, and refined aged wine."
—Isaiah 25:6, *NASB*

Chapter 17
Describing Your Dining Experience

*a*fter completing your detailed study, you are now ready to describe from your own palate what you tasted in the meal: write a few sentences which describe what the book was about from your personal viewpoint. When you were analyzing each chapter, you were required to make an outline by listing the main points in each chapter. This outline should be your own insight into God's Word, including any observations you gained from spending time with God at the dinner table.

Review all of your information to see what was put on your spiritual plate. Once you have digested each meal, you will want to get into the habit of asking yourself questions to see if you have obtained any new knowledge of the book you just read.

- What were the principal *ingredients*—the subject or theme?
- What insight did I gain from the *appetizers*—the specific words—used in this meal?
- Have I chosen a *salad* that I really enjoyed dining on—a verse to put to memory?
- How do the *entrées*—the chapters—taste together as a meal? What points were brought out when I put them together? How can these truths now transform my mind and change my life?
- What have I learned from the *desserts*—the characters?
- What does this chapter teach me about Jesus, *the Main Secret Ingredient?*

- Are there any *Healthy Dietary* choices I can make—that is, examples for me to follow?

- Were there any *Weight-Loss* tips—that is, sins or errors I can avoid?

- Are there any *Exercising* duties—that is, commands for me to perform?

- Are there any *after-dinner mints* or *sweet treats* of promises or blessings for me to claim after I meet any conditions?

- Does this meal contain any *seasoning*—that is, prayers I can use to enhance the quality of my life?

When you answer these questions, you will not only feed your soul, but come to a better understanding of the meal you have eaten. Now you have the knowledge to share your spiritual dining experience with someone else!

Chapter 18

Your Spiritual Fitness Program

*"Do you not know that you are the temples of God and that
the Spirit of God dwells in you? . . . For the temple is holy,
which temple you are."*
—1 Corinthians 3:16–17

Chapter 18
Your Spiritual Fitness Program

Society has us constantly fixating on our physical bodies and appearance. But as children of God, Christ Jesus would have us focus more on our spiritual bodies in which the Spirit of God resides. Rather than seeking to please men, He would have us become a pleasing sight to Him. It is the spiritual body that most reflects His image. Yet, for some believers, the spiritual body is the most neglected. This is sad. After all, the physical body is going to get old and perish one day, but the spiritual body is going to live for eternity—either in the presence of God or without it.

God wants our temples to be perfect and complete in Him, lacking nothing (James 1:4). That's why we need to get on a good spiritual fitness program. This will require us to lose weight, eat right, and exercise—that is, to shed sin, apply the Word of God in our lives, and walk according to God's will and purpose for each one of us.

The Spiritual Fitness Program in this devotional cookbook will help you do your part to fit into the image of a true believer in Jesus Christ. Don't worry if the task seems too big for you—you've got a personal fitness trainer, the Holy Spirit, to keep you going and accomplish the work in you.

To get on a spiritual fitness plan, as you study, you'll need to list any personal insights that God has revealed to you to apply to your life.

The Weight-Loss Program

You may not have been aware of it, but you've already been developing your own list of "foods" to avoid in this Weight-Loss Program. You have written down sins committed by the characters in the Bible which will give you knowledge of what to avoid. If you've been dining with the King, you'll also become aware of contaminated foods in your own spiritual body—that is, sins you've been harboring or temptations you've been playing with, foods that carry trans-fats, bitter herbs, and spiritual food poisoning. Trans fats—spiritually, sins—are far more lethal than we realize because they have the ability to reduce the level of good in us. We can be spiritually overweight because of a high sin intake, which contributes to such conditions as spiritual heart disease and spiritual death.

We are faced with many different challenges in our lives. To move us in the right direction, we need to eliminate the trans-fats and bitter herbs from our diets and consider an alternative menu that contains zero grams of fat to work out for our good, and in turn, give God glory. As you learn more about sin in the study of Scripture, you will need to eliminate sinful "foods" from your system in order to have a healthy heart and spiritual body fit for the continuance of an intimate relationship with God.

The Healthy Dietary Program

As you know if you've ever been on a physical diet, eating right isn't just about eliminating fats and other dangerous foods. It's also about eating *good* ones. The Bible is full of "spiritual proteins" that supply energy and help us maintain a healthy heart and spiritual body. You are on a program of mind transformation according to Romans 12:1: you are committing to a conscious effort to change.

As you study, list the life-changing behaviors, attitudes, habits, personalities, characteristics, and practices you find written, commanded, and exemplified in the Bible. These are the foods you should be indulging in to improve the quality of your life for God and for those whom you love. Feed on the good things of the Word of God, and take the time and effort to apply them to your life.

The Exercise Program

Every good food program includes a healthy exercise routine to keep us in shape. The more we exercise, the better we feel, and the less likely we are to become weak and sickly. God requires us to exercise when He ask us to "walk" in His ways (teachings) so He can get our temples in perfect shape.

In this book, a 6-Step Starter Program has been designed for you to begin stimulating and building up certain areas of your spiritual body, making you a pleasing sight to God and benefiting you. You'll soon have that spiritual six-pack that shows that your flabbiness caused by sin and disobedience is gone!

Exercising—that is, applying all you've learned in the Word— enables you to build up the muscles in your spiritual body each day. A true believer needs to perform the following exercises to keep every part of the spiritual body functioning to its fullest potential so we can flex those spiritual muscles and stay in step with God as we walk in daily obedience to Him.

STEP ONE:

Exercise Your Love for God and One Another

God commands us to love Him with all of our heart, soul, and strength (Deuteronomy 6:4). Since one of His attributes is love, He requires that we be fully in love with Him and that we show love for one another. In order to exercise our love for Him, we must learn how He expects to be loved.

Love Is What We Do

When we really love someone, he or she is always on our mind. We always want to be in that person's presence, with a constant flow of communication. We enjoy the company of our loved one, and we express our love when we give of ourselves, as well as by doing things that will please the other person. We tend to put our loved ones before ourselves. We have beautiful thoughts about them throughout the day, and we even go to the point of telling others about how wonderful they are. We bring our loved ones gifts on special occasions to show our love for them. They are a reason we smile. Take note: God has done all these things for us first before He asked us to do them for Him.

If we, as humans, know how to show our love for those whom we love so much, how much more is it to show our love for the One who first loved us? Love is not only what we *feel,* but is, basically, what we *do.* After all, God the Father demonstrated His great love for us when He did something that none of us would have done; He gave His *only* begotten Son, Jesus Christ, to die in our place. Then Jesus, God the Son, showed how much He loved us by doing something I doubt any one of us would have done, especially for a stranger or someone who hates and rejects us: He demonstrated His love for us by dying on the cross for our sins while we were yet sinners. And then there is God the Holy Spirit: He descended from heaven to reside in us sinful creatures, just to show us how much He loves us too. I know none of us would have wanted to give up living in a plush residency just to live in all of our small, one-room dwellings and endure our sinful ways that cause Him to grieve over us!

God also shows His love when He exercises with us. He exercises His lovingkindness, justice, and righteousness here on earth, and He delights in us when we exercise with Him. We exercise our lovingkindness when we boast in our understanding and knowledge of Him while here on earth. Jeremiah 9:24b: "I am the Lord who exercises lovingkindness, justice and righteousness on earth" (NASB).

Believers in Jesus Christ are the "apple of His eye" because we are the special object of His love, as we can see from all that He has done for us. I stand in awe at the mysteries of His love! God's love and grace amaze me when He takes notice of us and is concerned about our actions and our daily affairs. He evens visits us as a friend would visit another friend, just to come by and talk. We see how interested He is in us when we read Psalm 8:4, which says, "What is man that You are mindful of him, and the son of man that you visit him? For You have made him a little lower than the angels, and You have crowned him with glory and honor."

The flavors of God's love are expressed throughout the Bible, and He desires to be loved by us the same way in return. First John 3:1 talks about how great is the love the Father has lavished on us, that we should be called children of God, and that He has given us the privilege of calling Him "Abba Father" because of His love for us (Mark 14:36, Romans 8:15, and Galatians 4:6). Love is the expression of God's personality. God does not merely love us, but

He *is* love . . . it is His very nature. God's love for us is manifested as He provides for our every need—physical, moral, mental, emotional, spiritual, and financial.

God most definitely should be the first and foremost supreme object of our love. He states this fact in the very first Ten Commandments to us. He must be loved with all of the heart, mind, soul, and strength. God expressed His love for us in the same way according to Jeremiah 32:41: "with all of His heart and all of His soul." He first loved us before He asked us to love Him first.

Our love for God is shown by keeping His commandments (see Exodus 20:6, 1 John 5:3, and 2 John 1:6). Love is the highest expression of God in His relation to us, so it must be *our* highest expression in our relationship to our Lord as well. "Love God with all your heart, soul and strength" (Deuteronomy 11:13).

Love Is What We Do . . . For Each Other

God commands us to love one another as He has loved us. The way God loves us is a perfect example of how we are to love each other. God has placed the Holy Spirit within us so that we can build one another up in love (Ephesians 4:16); therefore, we should never tear one another down. To love one another means that regardless of how we feel or what we think about one another, we will accept each other just as we are (faults and all) and be willing to serve and to do for each other. Love is excellent because it has the power to forgive, heal, tolerate, encourage, endure, save, bind, and empower the believer. *Love* never fails. It covers a multitude of sins (1 Corinthians 13:8 and 1 Peter 4:8).

Scripture teaches that he who loves God will love his brother—that is, every believer—also (1 John 4:20). The degree to which we are to love one another is "as yourself" (Matthew 22:39). We should treat each other the way we want others to treat us.

The love we are to manifest toward one another is beautifully expressed in 1 Corinthians 13: "Love is patient, love is kind, and is not jealous; love does not brag and is not arrogant, does not act unbecomingly, it does not seek its own, is not provoked, does not take into account a wrong suffered, does not rejoice in unrighteousness, but rejoices with the truth, bears all things, believes all things, hopes all things, endures all things" (NASB). Notice also that God loves us in the same way. He faithfully rejoices the same way over us simply because His love never fails us.

Moreover, we cannot overlook the fact that God has also commanded His children to love their enemies; those who speak evil of us and despitefully use us (Matthew 5:43–48). Love is more than just mere affection. It manifests itself in our obedience to God, which is for our protection and defense, because those who love God will hate evil and sin (not the sinner) and all forms of worldliness as it is expressed in the lust of the eyes, the lust of the flesh, and the pride of life (Psalm 97:10, 1 John 2:15–17). In every relationship we have in life, we are to honor God in it.

STEP TWO:
Exercise Your Faith in God (Not in Man)

God tells us in His Word that without faith, it is impossible to please Him (Hebrews 11:6). He wants us to be totally dependent on Him and no one else. (You will taste and experience the flavors and aromas of faith when you dine on the book of Habakkuk and learn how important it is that we live by faith and not by sight!) Exercising our faith is a visible expression of our trust in God, because faith is the primary idea of trust. It is the full assurance, in accordance with the evidence, on which trust rests. Faith in Christ secures the believer's freedom from condemnation. It gives us the freedom to participate in a life that is in Christ Jesus, and it gives us peace with God (Romans 5:1).

One of the Bible's most famous definitions of faith is found in Hebrews 11:1, which states, "Now faith is the substance of things hoped for, the evidence of things not seen." Most of us know what we are hoping for, but have you ever thought about the "evidence of things not seen"? When God delivered the nation of Israel from slavery in Egypt, He proved to them through signs and wonders that they could trust totally in Him. However, the Israelites ignored, forgot, or often missed the evidence. We do the same today. Why do we miss what God is doing? Mainly because we lack the knowledge of God that we should be receiving in a daily walk with Him as we exercise in His ways.

God provides us with evidence that is seen and heard, through His signs and wonders (deeds) that pass by our very eyes and ears each day, to prove that He is in control of everything. (Romans 1:19) Just take a good look at creation, and read and watch the things happening today that relate to the things God tells us to watch for regarding the end times. Sometimes you'll discern things that give evidence of God working to answer your prayers by lining up circumstances that turn out in your favor and for your good, just to show you that you can totally trust Him with your life as you follow Him "to the Promise Land". However, you must stay in fellowship with constant communication (prayer) so God can speak to you and show you things as you walk with Him "through the wilderness".

Evidence is an outward sign or indication that furnishes proof or testimony; it is something that allows us to ascertain the truth of a matter. Webster's Dictionary also states that evidence implies the presence of visible signs, which serve as indications of a person's intention or state of mind, or of the probable nature of a past or coming event.

Being that faith is the substance of things hoped for and the evidence of things unseen, we should *consider the things we hope for* and then start *looking and listening for the visible evidence* that God provides as we listen to His voice or read His Word. He offers us great evidence to help us hear and see that He can be trusted and is working behind the scenes on our behalf, and He shows it to us so that we might know who He is when we step out on faith. (Deuteronomy 4:35: "To you it was shown, that you might know that the Lord Himself is God; there is none other besides Him.")

Be careful not to "half-step," causing the Holy Spirit to grieve. Trusting the Holy Spirit to teach and guide you is the other half of every step you must take so that the Holy Spirit can stomp out the sin in your life and transform you into God's image and likeness.

If we believe that our steps have been ordered by God, then we know that everything we experience has been allowed by God and will turn out for our good and for His glory. Hallelujah!

The more time you spend talking with God, the more you will get to know Him. The more you know Him, the more you will trust and depend on Him. The more you walk with Him, the more you will grow in love with Him. So keep on stepping by walking in faith!

STEP THREE:
Exercise Your Obedience to Know God's Will for Your Life

The opposite of ignorance is not knowledge, as we might expect. Instead, the opposite of ignorance is *obedience.* If we gain knowledge and yet choose not to act on it, what have we really learned? We are still considered ignorant. Our actions—or the lack of them—are no different from the actions of those who do not know Christ. Our walk isn't just about how much we understand about God's Word, but about how much of God's Word we apply to our lives. God's Word bears fruit only when it is applied. To be truly healthy spiritually, we must exercise obedience.

Our loyalty to God is reflected in our obedience. Obedience should be one of our most outstanding characteristics as believers in Christ Jesus (1 Samuel 15:22: "To obey is better than sacrifice").

As Christ humbled Himself, becoming obedient to His Father's will, we too must humble ourselves to become obedient to God, seeking not our own will in the process, but the will of our heavenly Father. At times this may feel frightening, but remember—do not fear, but instead walk by faith. We can trust that the will of God will never take us where His grace will not protect us.

Obedience is the guiding principle by which we must operate in our Father's work: the work of the ministry, preaching the good news, making disciples, and edifying the body of the church. Obedience is also the supreme test of faith in God, as well as reverence toward Him. Obedience holds the believer close to God, because it is a necessary condition for a right relationship with God to be sustained. Our blessings and prosperity are conditioned on our obedience to God (Isaiah 1:19: "If you are willing and obedient, you shall eat the good of the land"). The Scriptures tell us that God tests us so that He can do *good* for us in the end. (Deuteronomy 8:16, NASB: "He might test, to do good for you in the end.")

On the other hand, fear can cause disobedience and brings about our distress, misfortune, calamity, famine, and spiritual death, and in some cases, physical death. Disobedience can also be the end result of fear, worry, anxiety, and sin. Disobedience is a rejection of the will of God, a refusal to hear or believe Him. Fear comes from Satan to cause you to disobey God when He has commanded you to exercise with Him in His ways (teachings). In disobedience, we have hardened our hearts and become stubborn, which causes us to disregard God's authority and rulership. Fear causes our disobedience to God, so don't let fear keep you from exercising your faith and obedience to God.

Christ is our greatest illustration of obedience. Scripture tells us that He humbled Himself all the way to death on the cross, becoming a living sacrifice for us. Philippians 2:8 tells us, "And being found in appearance as a man, He humbled Himself by becoming obedient to the point of death, even death on a cross." Our union with Christ is in our obedience through faith as we become His disciples. We are called to be imitators of Christ. Being our perfect example, Christ never asks us to do anything that He has not already done Himself.

In imitating Christ, we too must become obedient and humble ourselves all the way to death to self, presenting ourselves as a living and holy sacrifice in order to prove what the will of God is for us, which is our reasonable spiritual service of worship (Romans 12:1).

You can begin to present yourself holy before the Lord by taking these necessary steps:

- Analyze and deal with your motives and the results of those motives by asking the question, "Why should I obey God?"
- Analyze and deal with your attitude and your actions by asking, "How should I obey God?"

The Holy Spirit is always reminding us, all throughout the Bible, not to fear because He is always with us, and every time He says

"Do not fear," what He is implying is to have faith and obey because He is there with us to guide us in our attitudes and actions as we obey God.

To exercise our obedience, we must condition our minds to listen for the voice of God that speaks to our hearts, and then we should follow the instructions we receive from Him.

Our relationship with God determines whether or not we know His voice. Through daily time with God, we can learn to know His voice when He speaks to us. It's the same as when you recognize a familiar voice in a crowd or on the other end of a telephone. You are familiar with the sound because you've had constant communication with that person. John 10:3–4 tells us, "And the sheep hear his voice; and he calls his own sheep by name and leads them out . . . and the sheep follow him, for they know his voice. Yet they will by no means follow a stranger, but they will flee from him, for they do not know the voice of strangers."

So now let me ask you this question: is Satan's voice strange or familiar to you? When you hear him speaking to you, do you "by no means" listen to his voice, or do you obey by following his suggestions or bad advice? God states in His Word that we are to be transformed by the renewing of our minds (Romans 12:2). We need to be obedient to the voice of God so that we can:

- Live in the will of God by living out God's purpose for our lives
- Do the will of God even when it contradicts our own ("Nevertheless not my will, but Yours, be done" Luke 22:42b)
- Be obedient to God; keep from sinning against God and man
- Become humble and grateful

- Have peace and unity with God and man

Like Jesus, you must learn how to use your sword or knife (God's Word) to defeat the enemy, and then you will have the strength to exercise your right to demand that Satan flee "because greater is He who is in you than he who is in the world" (1 John 4:4).

STEP FOUR:
Exercise Our Forgiveness Toward One Another

God commands us to forgive one another as He has forgiven us. Forgiveness implies a release: it is to set a person free (Ephesians 4:31–32). It is the dismissal or suspension of a just penalty or guilt.

Real forgiveness does not set up conditions that must be met before forgiveness is given. After all, God forgave us long before we ever knew Him, while we were still sinners who had rejected Him. He did this freely without setting up any preconditions for us to fulfill. His forgiveness was expressed before the foundation of the world when He made plans for our salvation.

Forgiveness is necessary in the body of Christ to avoid discord and division among believers. Unforgiveness causes pain and suffering that can directly or indirectly affect everyone in the body of Christ. It affects our fellowship with God and with one another. Yes, it is sometimes painful to forgive, but God does not give us any other option to relieve the bitterness that will destroy us if we hold on to it. (Forgiveness can be sweet for the forgiver as well as the forgiven once you forgive).

When we have a toothache, this one little part of the body can cause enough pain to indirectly affect the entire body. Sometimes it feels like our entire body is hurting, and until we obtain relief from this painful situation, we can't function properly. If we refuse to administer the pain relief of forgiveness toward one another, it can have a great negative effect on all those involved and ultimately hurt the entire church body. You can also make yourself physically sick when you harbor anger too long toward anyone and choose not to forgive. On the other hand, forgiveness can overcome a lifetime of pain and anger for the forgiver.

STEP FIVE:
Exercise Our Prayers to Communicate with God

Prayer is simply addressing or conversing directly with God. It is our means of communication with God in the supernatural realm. It allows us to access God's power and gives us victory in the natural realm. Prayer also trains the soul to focus on the Lord.

There are several areas to consider when praying to God:

- *Prayers of Understanding:* It is important to pray before, during, and after your daily study of the Word, or whenever you feel the urge to "season your food" and gain a better understanding of God's Word and purpose for your life because everybody's taste (level of understanding) is different, based on how much they have eaten (digested). We should also pray this type of prayer concerning decisions, both major and minor, and wait on the Lord to direct our paths before we act. This will keep us from acting on impulse, causing regret when we make hasty decisions.

- *Prayers of Thanksgiving:* After dining at the table of God's Word, we should exercise a prayer of thanksgiving. End every "meal" with prayer, and find something specific in it that you can be thankful for in order to compliment the Master Chef, Jesus Christ, when you sing God a new song of praise. This type of prayer is one that should be constant throughout our days. When you take into consideration what is going on in your life and how you are secure in Christ Jesus, give thanks!

It is important to pray about everything, regardless of how large or how small. We want to become totally dependent on God to direct and guide us in every situation and circumstance. He wants to hear from us on a regular basis about everything that concerns us because the heart of our prayers meets the Heart of God.

The exercise of prayer also goes hand-in-hand with the exercise of obedience. We call God our Lord, but we need to let Him *be* Lord over every area of our lives.

STEP SIX:
Exercise Your Spiritual Gifts for the Building Up of God's Kingdom

To exercise our spiritual gifts is to exercise our skills and abilities in the church. Using our spiritual gifts is also a form of worship to God. Romans 12:1 tell us to "present your bodies a living sacrifice, holy, acceptable unto God, which is your reasonable service."

For us to be holy means that our bodies must be set apart for God and put to holy use. Because you gave your life to Christ, you belong to God to use for His glory. To be acceptable, we should labor to be accepted of the Lord and to please Him well in and out of church. Our reasonable service is just that—reasonable—because He has equipped us for every good work. God does not impose upon us anything that is too hard or unreasonable, even though for some, much is given and much is required (Luke 12:48). He simply says to us, as He said to Isaiah in Isaiah 6:8, "Whom should I send, and who will go for Us?" Isaiah's response was, "Here am I! Send me."

How you are going to respond to God's call is an individual decision. When you act on your commitment to God, it creates a deeper devotion to Jesus; so exercise your spiritual gifts by providing dedicated service and serve with love. (Romans 12:6-21)

If you have problems committing to God as you serve in His kingdom, then you should ask God to reveal the things that prevent you from committing your time, talents, and treasures to Him. The answers may not be easy to take. But if you want to be spiritually fit, you've got to exercise.

Chapter 19

Dancing with the King

*"He guides me in the paths of righteousness
for His name sake"*
—Psalm 23:3

*"But when He, the Spirit of truth comes,
He will guide you into all the truth..."*
—John 16:13

*"The Lord alone guided him,
And there was no foreign god with him."*
—Deuteronomy 32:12

Chapter 19

Dancing with the King:

A Special Exercise Treat for Steppin' In The Name of the Lord

*O*ne of the greatest exercises for the physical and spiritual body is to dance. You get to move all of your spiritual muscles when you dance with the King. While at the banquet feast, God will want you to dance with Him. "Dancing with the King" is all about *guidance.* This is when we allow the King to guide us through His Word and keep us in His will for our lives as we follow His ways.

When we take a look at the word *guidance,* we see *G, U, I,* and *dance*—the word says, "God, You and I dance." The order in which the letters appear clearly indicates who takes the lead as we dance together! God knows all the right moves to make and all the right steps to take to keep us in perfect sync with whatever tune is playing in our lives. Sometimes the beats are slow and easy to dance to; at other times, they are fast and hard to keep in step—especially without His guidance.

If we take the lead, we will find ourselves stepping on the King's toes. With our rhythm off and our steps out of sync with the King, we may even fall down. We must allow the King to guide us in the right direction so that the melody of life will be sweet for us while dancing with the King. It feels so good when we are in harmony and perfect step with the King! So the next time you get a choice to either sit it out or dance…I hope you dance and give the heavens and the world an opportunity to glance at you dancing with the King. Grab hold of God's hand as He guides you through every situation, and *keep steppin' in the name of the Lord.*

Chapter 20

Becoming a Spiritual Connoisseur

"According to my earnest expectation and hope
that in nothing I shall be ashamed, but with all boldness,
as always, so now also Christ will be magnified in my body,
whether by life or by death."
—*Philippians 1:20*

Chapter 20
Becoming a Spiritual Connoisseur

*W*hen you leave the dinner table of God's Word every day, you can expect to:

- Develop the ability to handle Scripture with self-confidence and without fear
- Come away with the experience and joy of personal discoveries of truths you never knew existed!
- Gain a deeper knowledge of Christ
- Develop a closer relationship with God
- Have the ability to exercise the power given you through the Holy Spirit
- Have the ability to share what you have learned

Over time, you will become a spiritual connoisseur. You can go anywhere in the world and will understand what you are expected to do, because the meals of God's Word are profitable for:

- *Doctrine and teaching.* The Word structures our thinking so we can think, live, and behave correctly.
- *Reproof or Rebuke.* The Word structures our lives and sets up boundaries to inform us of sin and God's standards for our lives.
- *Instruction and Correction.* The Word provides purification and cleansing of the sin in our lives to conform us to the will of God.

- *Righteous and Profitable living.* When we learn to live according to the Word and follow its guidelines, we can live a successful and abundant lifestyle.

2 Timothy 3:16 – "All scripture is given by inspiration of God, and is profitable for doctrine, for reproof, for correction for instruction in righteousness." (NASB)

Prayerfully, take the time to study and master God's Word. You will learn:

1. Who you are in Christ Jesus
2. What your responsibilities are as a believer
3. What you should and should not do as a child of God
4. What it means to be chosen of God
5. How you are sanctified by the Spirit in love
6. What it means to be covered by the blood of Jesus Christ
7. That you are a subject of grace and have the possession of peace
8. What your privileges are as a friend of Jesus
9. What your calling is as a bondservant of God
10. What security, joy, and hope you have in the All-Sufficient One
11. All of the possibilities, suffering, trials, and dangers that are before you
12. What it means to be in warfare with your spiritual enemy and how to win the battle for your good and God's glory

As a spiritual connoisseur, you can tell anyone the good news without fear. You know that you have been saved and equipped to serve God's meals with excitement and enthusiasm. Because of your boldness, you are expected to receive from God your personal assignment with gladness since you have personally tasted all of God's meals and were abundantly successful while dining with the King.

All you have learned is to equip you for every good work in Christ. The meals of the Bible will enable you to become an effective servant of our Lord and Savior, Jesus Christ.

The knowledge you gain creates responsibility. The moment you learn of God's truths, it is your responsibility to act on them. Application is the most neglected, but the most needed process of spiritual growth and maturity. Welcoming the truth into your life means *doing* something as a result of what you have learned from your study. As you become more and more a connoisseur of the Word, you will develop into the Christlike image of our heavenly Father.

Remember that God loves you, Christ died for you, and the Holy Spirit has gifted and empowered you.

It's Not Just for You

As a spiritual connoisseur, you are responsible to properly display the image of God to others. You can show appreciation and dedication for becoming a spiritual connoisseur through a commitment to service. You are a bondservant of God; which means you have a permanent relation of servitude to God, and His desire is for you to serve others in His name. As a bondservant you will be tastefully consumed in the will of the Master Chef and your goal in life will be to serve the Master's dishes to the children in His house and to all those who stand outside the door of God's house begging for His spiritual soup to sooth their sin sick souls. Jesus came to earth to serve, not to sit and you are to do likewise; to serve, not sit. (John 17:18 says, "In the same way that you gave Me a mission in the world, I give them a mission in the world." – MSG) Your mission is not impossible, if you chose to accept it; is to provide quality service—those you serve should always come first. Take responsibility for this work. Finally, use and develop good judgment by analyzing, evaluating, and carefully applying the Word of God in every situation.

You will become a positive, influential person in the lives of others as you acquire the skills and knowledge necessary to succeed in this lifelong journey of service. You will have the ability to create an environment among believers where everyone feels valued and encouraged to use their spiritual gifts to edify the body of Christ. I can personally testify that my church made me feel like I belonged, and the more I served God's people, the more valuable I became in edifying the body of Christ. I received encouragement to use my spiritual gifts that brought an atmosphere of enthusiasm.

I encourage you to recognize your value to your ministry and use your spiritual gifts for God, because He did not save you and give you these gifts for you to sit down on them. You were saved and gifted to serve them to others. Your spiritual gifts are to be used to the edification of the body of Christ for His glory and honor through your life of service. Not only that, but these gifts did not come with an expiration date on them. I personally wear a "chef's coat of humility" as a spiritual sous chef and connoisseur to serve in the Master Chef's universal kitchen, serving up His specially prepared meals that He wants you to dine on every day. Being that I'm just an ordinary person serving the extraordinary Master Chef's meals; if I can do it, so can you.

There is a wide range of possibilities for your service as you become a spiritual connoisseur who studies to show yourself approved unto God, a <u>workman</u> who needs not to be ashamed, but rightly divides the truth (2 Timothy 2:15). You are becoming a spiritual culinary professional, not ashamed of the gospel, but using your spiritual culinary gifts and skills in various ways as you serve many portions of spiritual food to others. Your skills may be used in private settings for fine dining in Bible study classrooms. You might use your expertise by providing room service to hospitals or convalescent patients. You may provide banquet hall service in congregational settings, or carryout food service to home study groups. You may even develop a seven-star complete service to a restaurant of ministries or offer institutional catering to correctional facilities.

As you go out of your way to satisfy your spiritual cravings, indulging in favorite Scriptures and enjoying an abundance of the after-dinner mints and sweet treats (promises and blessings) God has so faithfully prepared for you, I believe in my heart that it will be a sweet treat for God to hear you telling others about the intimate meals you have with Him. What a joy to be able to tell someone that you've had several "helpings" of specially prepared cuisine, spiritual gourmet food prepared by your personal "Master Chef" Himself, that was waiting for you when you got home.

I encourage you to use some of this culinary terminology as you speak of your experiences in Bible study. As you express your excitement over the fantastic meals you've had while dining with the King, I can imagine the look of surprise on the faces of others as they realize that you are really talking about studying the Word of God! This just might be a door of opportunity for you to walk through and be used by God in the life of someone who has never tasted God's "recipes." Perhaps you can encourage one of your brothers or sisters in Christ to consider making their own dinner reservations for two when they see how excited you are about dining with the King every day.

Spiritual connoisseurs allow their lives to tell the world about their knowledge of Christ, their commitment to Him, and their strong beliefs in the Son of God. They can answer the question Jesus asked His disciples when He said, "Who do you say that I am?" (Matthew 16:15). They know that it is a privilege to be used by God, and they are eager and excited to help in God's universal kitchen to send out portions of spiritual food to the masses. In fact, they look forward to assisting the Master Chef in many fresh and exciting ways because they know they can make a difference in the world. It is perfectly fine with them if someone mistakes them for "the help," because they are always helping others by serving "Soup" (witnessing and evangelizing) to the lost and serving others in the body of Christ by (discipling) the saved as they help themselves by dining on the many flavorful dishes found at the greatest and largest banquet table: the Word of God. (Esther 9:22b, NASB: "They should make them days of feasting and rejoicing and sending portions of food to one another and gifts to the poor.")

A Personal Recipe From
§ The Spiritual Gourmet Chef's Kitchen §

Have you been studying to show yourself approved unto God?
Then treat yourself to a special treat created by your Spiritual
Gourmet Chef.

Dessert Recipe

Adam's Apple & Eve's Raisin Cobbler

6 large Red Delicious apples (peeled & sliced)
1 cup raisins
¼ teaspoon cinnamon
¼ teaspoon nutmeg
2 sticks butter
2 tablespoons vanilla extract
½ cup sugar
Lemon juice

Crust
2 lb. butter
12 oz. sugar
1 tsp. salt
2 eggs
2 cups pastry flour (sifted)
Cold water

Preheat oven to 375º. Melt 1 lb of butter in a small saucepan. Add sugar, cinnamon, nutmeg, and water. Bring to a boil, stirring until the sugar is dissolved. Remove from heat and add vanilla.

Toss the sliced apples gently with lemon juice to keep the apples from turning brown. Spread the apples evenly in a 12 x 20-inch baking pan, and mix in raisins. Pour sauce over apples and raisins.

Roll out flour dough and slice evenly into strips. Place dough strips over the apples first vertically and then horizontally.

Melt remaining ½ cup of butter and pour over dough. Lightly sprinkle dough with sugar to add flavor, and place in oven.

Baking time: 45 minutes or until crust is a golden to medium brown.

Note: If possible, use a stainless steel pan instead of an aluminum pan. The acid of the fruit will react with the aluminum and create an undesirable flavor.

Be Fruitful & Take Dominion!

Chapter 21

A Word to God's Healthy Eaters

*"Beloved, I pray that you may prosper in all things
and be in health, just as your soul prospers."*
—3 John 1:2

Chapter 21
A Word to God's Healthy Eaters

*P*hysically healthy eaters are encouraged to eat three meals a day, and they don't skip a meal. They eat breakfast, lunch, and dinner every day. I encourage you to do the same spiritually. According to society, breakfast is the most important meal of the day. If that's the case, then eating a spiritual breakfast will bless you also because it starts your day off right. It is the best or choicest meal of the day, considering that it's the firstfruit, the beginning—the first in place, time, order, or rank—and it is God's provision for us so we can give Him the firstfruits of our day in prayer, praise, and reading His Word. It will also hold you over until you can eat another spiritual meal.

A spiritual breakfast is important because a word from God early in the morning will guide you and keep you when you need it the most. You should at least eat your spiritual "breakfast bar" (read one chapter in the morning) before starting off your day. Jesus even encouraged His disciples to eat breakfast with Him. (John 21:12 – "Jesus said to them, *'Come and have breakfast.'"*)

For lunch, while dining on your physical food, allow your spirit to eat a good healthy lunch also by serving it a variety of spiritual salads. Take out your "lunch box" with the special selections of salads (memory verses) you wrote down to memorize and give your spirit a chance to be blessed by some choice dining so you can begin to apply the verses to your life while eating lunch with God.

For dinner, you can dine in by keeping your dinner reservations with the King and studying His Word at home or you can go out to eat by attending a Bible study for a change in your dining room atmosphere.

Healthy eaters receive their daily blessings by eating their daily bread because they are disciplined, faithful, and obedient in reading and studying the Word of God. They are always hungry and thirsty. They know how and what to eat in order to satisfy their hunger and thirst for righteousness. Their number one motive and objective is to please the King, the One and Only True and Living God.

Whether you use the Royal Candlelight study guides or read the Bible on your own, once you've completed the "meals" of God's Word by studying them all once through, don't stunt your spiritual growth and maturity in Christ by not continuing to feed yourself wholesome meals on a regular basis. I recommend that you read other books on Bible study and theology and/or enroll in Bible study classes designed to offer you a greater and deeper relationship with God.

The Royal Candlelight Culinary Book Series offers you four more "Spiritual Recipe Books" to help you become a healthy eater of God's Word. Work on your spiritual culinary skills by taking the opportunity to dine with us on all sixty-six books of the Bible under the Royal Candlelight. The Royal Candlelight Recipe Books are prepared as four-course meals fit for royalty, using workbook-style, highly personalized "recipes" similar to the sample study you read in chapter 16. All four spiritual culinary recipe books are structured to bring every prince and princess in the royal family of God to a higher standard of godly living. Listed here for your enjoyment of God's fantastic meals is a brief description of each follow-up spiritual recipe book (study guides) written for godly living.

Dining By Royal Candlelight offers *spiritual fine-dining for the true believer of God.* These in-depth studies cover specially selected books of the Old and New Testaments which consist of one to six chapters each. This spiritual recipe book will teach you the proper etiquette and fine dining techniques required as you dine at the King's banquet table while dining by the true "Royal Candlelight"— the Light of Jesus Christ! This book covers twenty-seven short books of the Bible and will be a good book to start off with if you want to dine on each meal in one sitting. From both the Old and New Testaments, the books covered are: *Ruth, Lamentations, Joel, Obadiah, Jonah, Nahum, Habakkuk, Zephaniah, Haggai, Malachi, Galatians, Ephesians, Philippians, Colossians, 1 & 2 Thessalonians, 1 & 2 Timothy, Titus, Philemon, James, 1 & 2 Peter, 1, 2 & 3 John, and Jude.*

The Royal Candlelight and You offers *spiritual gourmet cuisine for the true believer of God.* These recipes consist of upscale "cuisines" selected from the New Testament, focusing on the characteristics and attributes of the Son of God, Jesus Christ. As you dine on these gourmet meals, which have been prepared to teach you in depth about Jesus, you will also learn about His provisions and expectations for every prince and princess in the royal kingdom of God. This book covers the following ten books of the Bible, taken from the New Testament: *Matthew, Mark, Luke, John, Acts, Romans, 1 & 2 Corinthians, Hebrews, and Revelation.*

The Royal Candlelight Classic Lean Cuisines is full of *spiritually rich lean cuisines for the true worshiper of God.* This is an in-depth study of specially selected books from the Old Testament, offering nonfat recipes covering wisdom and prophesies to help you make wise decisions in your life as you prepare for your new royal lifestyle and what's to come of it. This book covers sixteen books of the Bible from the Old Testament: *Ezra, Esther,*

Job, Psalms, Proverbs, Ecclesiastes, Song of Solomon, Nehemiah, Isaiah, Jeremiah, Ezekiel, Daniel, Hosea, Amos, Micah, and Zechariah.

The Royal Candlelight Banquet Feasts is a book of *foundationally rich culinary cuisines for the King's royal children.* These spiritual recipes are in-depth studies of the first thirteen books of the Bible, which includes the foundation of mankind. This ultimate gourmet feast is not a natural taste for everyone, but once you acquire that taste, you'll relish it! It's just a tiny spoonful away from your total spiritual dining enjoyment. This book covers thirteen books of the Bible: *Genesis, Exodus, Leviticus Numbers, Deuteronomy, Joshua, Judges, 1 & 2 Samuel, 1 & 2 Kings, and 1 & 2 Chronicles.*

The Royal Candlelight Recipe Book Series will not only teach you how to study, but will allow you to feast on all sixty-six books of the Bible as you learn. The Royal Candlelight shines brightly from the center of the King's banquet table as these recipes illuminate the importance of dining sufficiently. The Master Chef, Jesus Christ, has prepared this great banquet from the best food to nourish and strengthen every child of God. You will not perish due to your lack of knowledge. You will, however, taste and see that the Lord is truly good—to you and for you!

At the time you read this, all four recipe books may not yet be in print. If you are interested in any of these future publications, please log on to our Christian Publishing Company website at www.royalcandlelight.com and view all of the published books written by your Spiritual Gourmet Chef and other inspiring authors who are spreading the "good news" of the gospel. You can also log on to www.info@royalcandlelight.com and let us know that you want to be put on our company e-mail listing for notification when these recipe books are released for publication.

There are other great sources of information that will assist you in studying as you search for the truth. Some of my knowledge on how to study the Bible came from feasting on other theological studies, some of which I gladly share below. However, keep in mind that my greatest knowledge first came from studying the Word of God.

Other Recommended Reading Materials
How to Study the Bible for Yourself by Tim LaHaye
Bible Study Methods by Rick Warren
How to Study the Bible for Greatest Profit by R.A. Torrey
Systematic Theology by Wayne Grudem

Don't forget when you feed your physical body that your spiritual body needs to eat too. It's much like having a set of twins: no good parent would feed one child and neglect or starve the other!

To paraphrase 1 Chronicles 28:8–9, where we receive wisdom given to the wisest man ever to walk the earth, King Solomon: we should be careful to seek out all the commandments of the Lord our God, so we too can possess this good land we are journeying through with Jesus by our side and the Holy Spirit abiding in us. As a good disciple, pass your wisdom on. God wants you to teach others; your sons and daughters and all those you are discipling who will come after you. Make disciples as you go into the highways (your homes, school, work, and neighborhoods); all the way to the ends of the earth. Remember you are not poor anymore. You are not like those who stand by the side of the road with their signs that say "I work for food." You are those the Master Chef has working for "eternal food" as stated in John 6:27; "Do not work for food which perishes, but for the food which endures to eternal life, which the Son of Man shall give to you, for on Him the Father, even God has set His seal."

"So now, in the sight of all Israel, the assembly of the LORD, and in the hearing of our God, observe and seek after all the commandments of the LORD your God so that you may possess the good land and bequeath IT to your sons after you forever. As for you, my son Solomon, know the God of your father, and serve Him with a whole heart and a willing mind; for the LORD searches all hearts, and understands every intent of the thoughts. If you seek Him, He will let you find Him; but if you forsake Him, He will reject you forever." (1 Chronicles 28:8–9; NASB)

Please remember that as authentic Christians, we must seek God with all our heart and mind. And don't forget that every time we sin or deliberately disobey God's commands, we stand before His presence and say, like Pharaoh did, "Who is the Lord that I should obey Him?" We forget that our heavenly Father sees everything, and we drag the Holy Spirit who resides in us into the presence of our very act of rebellion, deeply grieving Him. One day, we are going to stand before God during judgment, and to many of us He is going to ask that same question: "Who are you?" (Matthew 7:23). When you say "Lord, I . . ." He is going to say "Depart from me," because He never knew you either (intimately, that is).

Don't let those be the last words you hear from God. Instead, allow God the good pleasure in saying:

"Well done, my good and faithful servant."

And remember, prince and princess . . .

Keep a spiritual Knife and Fork handy at all times, because the best is yet to come when you dine on the Word of God for yourself.

These Meals Do the Spiritual Body Good.

Bon Appétit!
"Royalty in the Making"

A Personal Recipe From
§ The Spiritual Gourmet Chef's Kitchen §

*Your Spiritual Gourmet Chef has created this recipe to bless you
in your completion of this devotional cookbook.*

Stay Devoted to Dining on The Master Chef's Spiritual Meals
and
Thank You for Dining with Us.

Sweet Treat Recipe

Devotional Butter Cookies

1½ stick butter
8 oz cup sugar
1 egg
1 teaspoon vanilla extract
½ teaspoon salt
1 teaspoon baking soda
2 cups flour

Preheat oven to 375º. Have all ingredients at room temperature. Place butter, sugar, and salt in a mixing bowl. (For light cookies, cream until the mix is light and fluffy. For a dense, chewier cookie, cream only slightly.)

Add egg and vanilla extract and blend at a low speed. Sift in the flour and baking soda. Mix until the ingredients are combined.

Make all cookies uniform in size and thickness for even baking. Drop cookie dough on ungreased cookie sheet.

Baking time 8 to 10 minutes or until the edges turn a light, golden brown color.

Stay Devoted and Be Blessed!

Chapter 22

Study Forms:
Creating Your Own Spiritual Recipes

*"Do your best to present yourself to God as one approved,
a worker who does not need to be ashamed
and who correctly handles the word of truth
—2 Timothy 2:15 (NIV)*

Chapter 22

Study Forms: Creating Your Own Spiritual Recipes

*Y*ou can create your own spiritual "recipes" by using the study forms below. This is your opportunity to delve into the riches of your royal dinner. You can record all the wonderful discoveries from your dining experiences as you feast on the delicacies prepared by the Master Chef.

Study Forms:

Word and Term Study

Verse-to-Verse Study

Chapter Study (Analysis)

Character Study

Outlining the Principal Features of the Meal

Your Daily Bread Spiritual Journal

WORD AND TERM STUDY

"Test all things; hold fast what is good."
—1 Thessalonians 5:21

Word/Term:

_____

Scripture Reference:

_____

Resource Tools (Sharp Knife, Dinner and Salad Forks):
Use the Bible Dictionary and the Concordance to find out how the
word or term is used in the selected passage of scripture.

The Original Meaning of the Word/Term:

_____

_____

_____

_____

_____

How is it used in the text?

_____

_____

_____

_____

_____

Translation Comparison:
How Is the Word Used in Other Bible Translations?

Bible Translation:

_____

Meaning:

_____

_____

_____

_____

_____

Bible Translation:

_____

Meaning:

_____

_____

_____

_____

_____

Dictionary Meaning:

_____

_____

_____

_____

_____

VERSE-TO-VERSE STUDY

"Your word I have hidden in my heart,
that I might not sin against thee."
—*Psalm 119:11*

Resource Tools (Sharp Knife, Dinner Fork and Dinner Spoon):
*Use the concordance and the commentary to gain a greater
knowledge and clearer understanding of the verse(s) you selected to
study.*

Suggestion:

- Pay close attention to the verses that are ahead of and behind each verse you are studying.
- Compare verses by examining parallel passages of Scripture that give an account of the same event.
- Revisit the verse over and over again until you have gotten as much as you possibly can get out of it. Write down everything that is revealed to you as you dine on the Word.
- Keep a list of unanswered questions and unresolved issues for further study.

Verse:

_____

_____

A. What does this verse mean?

_____

_____

_____

_____

B. What does this verse teach me?

_____

_____

_____

_____

_____

_____

_____

_____

C. What are my questions and/or issues with this verse?

_____

_____

_____

_____

_____

_____

D. What are the answers to my questions and/or unresolved issues?

_____

_____

_____

_____

_____

_____

_____

CHAPTER STUDY

"Be diligent to present yourself approved to God,
a workman who does not need to be ashamed,
rightly dividing the word of truth"
—2 Timothy 2:15

Passage of Scripture: _____

Resource Tool (Sharp Knife)

Instructions:

- Identify the main idea or theme of the chapter, and then state it in a couple of words. Evaluate how the chapter, as a whole, relates to the rest of the book.

- Answer the following questions. *Focus on contrasts, similarities (words that are either opposite or similar to each other), and things that are repeated, related, emphasized, or true to the experiences of your own life.*

1. What does it say about Christ, and what name is used to describe Him in this chapter?

   _____

   _____

   _____

   _____

2. Who is speaking, who are they speaking to, and what is the reason or circumstance behind this chapter?

   _____

   _____

   _____

   _____

3. What are the main promises (if any) and what conditions are required to obtain these promises?

_____

_____

_____

_____

_____

4. Are there any commands or instructions to follow?

_____

_____

_____

_____

_____

5. Are there any errors made or sins committed that should be avoided?

_____

_____

_____

_____

_____

6. What have I observed in this chapter that challenges the way I live today?

_____

_____

_____

_____

_____

7. What do I need from this chapter to apply to my life today?

_____

_____

_____

_____

_____

8. Was there a prayer in this chapter that I need to echo?

_____

_____

_____

_____

_____

CHARACTER STUDY

"For the LORD gives wisdom;
from His mouth comes knowledge and understanding."
—*Proverbs 2:6*

Resource Tools: Study Bible (Sharp Knife), Commentary (Dinner Spoon) and Handbook (Salad Fork)

Name of Character: _____

Scripture Reference: _____

- What is the meaning of this character's name?

  _____

  _____

  _____

  _____

  _____

  _____

  _____

- Does the meaning of this character's name have any bearing on the passage of Scripture or the theme of the book?

  _____

  _____

  _____

  _____

  _____

_____

_____

- What are the elements of power and success that this
  character possesses or experiences?

  _____

  _____

  _____

  _____

  _____

  _____

  _____

- Does this character experience any elements of
  suffering, weakness, or failure? If so, what are they?

  _____

  _____

  _____

  _____

  _____

  _____

  _____

- Were there any difficulties this character had to
  overcome? If so, why?

  _____

  _____

  _____

  _____

  _____

  _____

- Do I see a type of Christ in this character? (That is, does this character show any characteristics of Jesus Christ?)

  _____

  _____

  _____

  _____

  _____

  _____

  _____

- Was this character obedient or disobedient to God? What were the consequences of the character's actions (good or bad)?

  _____

  _____

  _____

  _____

  _____

  _____

  _____

- Did this character commit a sin, neglect any opportunities presented, or make any mistakes that I need to take into consideration when examining his or her actions?

  _____

  _____

_____

_____

_____

_____

_____

_____

_____

_____

- What have I learned from this character that will help
  me in my relationship with Christ?

_____

_____

_____

_____

_____

_____

_____

_____

_____

_____

_____

_____

_____

*"Remember those who led you who spoke the word of God to you;
and considering the result of their conduct, imitate their faith."*
Hebrews 13:7 (NASB)

OUTLINING THE PRINCIPAL FEATURES OF YOUR STUDY
Completing Your Meal

"All scripture is given by inspiration of God, and is profitable for doctrine, for reproof, for correction, for instruction in righteousness."
—2 Timothy 3:16

NAME OF THE BOOK (The Meal):

_____

THEME (Main Features of the Meal) in one or two words or a phrase:

_____

_____

MAJOR POINTS (Qualities of the Meal): What practical issues does this book address?

- _____
- _____
- _____
- _____
- _____

THE CONCLUSION (Observation): What have I seen in this book?

_____

_____

_____

MY DINING EXPERIENCE (Interpretation): Personal Insight:

_____

_____

_____

_____

_____

SINS TO AVOID (Weight-Loss Program)_:_ What have I seen that challenges the way I live?

_____

_____

_____

_____

_____

PERSONAL LIFE-CHANGING APPLICATION (Healthy Dietary Program): What changes do I need to consider in light of the study?

_____

_____

_____

_____

_____

Note: Share the results of your study with someone you love.

YOUR DAILY BREAD SPIRITUAL JOURNAL

"I have treasured the words of His mouth
more than my necessary food."
—Job 23:12

Scripture _____   **Date:** _____

List the Royal Candlelight message you received from God today:

_____

_____

_____

_____

_____

List the After-Dinner Mint or Sweet Treat (Promise or Blessing) from God you were given:

_____

_____

_____

_____

_____

List the Condition that must be met to receive an After-Dinner Mint or Sweet Treat:

_____

_____

_____

List the Command(s) to Keep:

_____

_____

_____

_____

_____

List the Timeless Principle(s) you see in this passage:

_____

_____

_____

_____

_____

List Applications to your life (Exercise Program):

_____

_____

_____

_____

_____

Write Out Your Vitamins and Supplements (Praise and Worship Report):

_____

_____

_____

_____

_____

_____

"A Special Bowl of Stew"

Prepared for Damnation

The Recipe for Sin and Rejection

A Special Bowl of Stew Prepared for Damnation
The Recipe for Sin and Rejection

Since the Master Chef put all of His spices of love and sweet herbs of compassion into the Soup of Salvation and all of the sixty-six biblical meals prepared for all of His children to dine on; those who hate God and reject Him and His Son leave the Master Chef with no other choice but to deal with what He has left over, and that is His anger and wrath, which has been prepared in the special bowl of STEW (Souls Tasting Eternal Wrath), because the Master Chef doesn't like to waste anything that is created in His universal kitchen. The King prepared a special table which He has reserved to serve this special stew for all who choose to reject the Master Chef's plan of salvation that He served in His awesome meals and refused to sit with the King and dine at His banquet table.

There will be no need for the folks at this reserved table to season this stew with their prayers, because the King will not be there to hear them. There will be nothing sweet-smelling coming from those dining at this table that can sooth God because the only thing you will hear at this table will be moaning and complaining over this bitter-tasting meal. There is no love or compassion added, only bitterness from the herbs and spices of wickedness, sin, evil, disobedience, and rebellion that will come from the field of destruction Satan planted with seeds of unbelief. These bitter roots will cause many a world of trouble because they are too short to produce grace and will only become useless stems of ungodliness for this single meal. Hebrews 12:15-16 "See to it that no one comes short of the grace of God; that no root of bitterness springing up causes trouble, and by it many be defiled that there be no immoral or godless person like Esau, who sold his own birthright for a single meal." (Genesis 25: 30-34) The sound of complaints from those stewing over this meal will be from the gnashing of teeth because the stew is fire-hot and it burns them as they taste the bitterness while they eat.

You can generally tell if someone hates to cook because the food doesn't taste like there was any love put into it as they prepared it. God hated to prepare this dish, so you won't find any love or compassion put into it either. Since the Master Chef used all of His Aged Royal Wine (the Holy Spirit) at the King's banquet table feast, they won't be getting any of this wine served at the table. The only wine the Master Chef had left over to put in the stew was a cup of bitter wine made from His fury which He added to enhance the flavor of His hatred of sin and immorality; that will cause everyone at the table to fall (Zechariah 12:2: "Behold, I am going to make Jerusalem a cup that causes reeling to all people around. And 1 Thessalonians 2:16: "...with the result that they always fill up the measure of their sins. But wrath has come upon them to the utmost.") They will all drink the wine of the wrath of God, which is mixed in full strength in the cup of His anger (Revelation 14:10).

Those who hated the Master Chef, Jesus Christ, God's only begotten Son, are use to dishing out their rejection, so it seems only fair that the King give back what they dished out. They get to taste their own nasty cruelty and bitter hatred. This is a hard dish to swallow, but stew is usually served during hard times, and it can't get any harder for them than at this time because God's anger burns.

There are lots of spiritual meats and vegetables that are mentioned in God's Word that will be placed in the stew if you choose not to eat the Soup of Salvation and accept the invitation to dine at the banquet table to feast on God's wholesome meals, which are prepared to last until eternity.

Their Last Supper

The stew has been simmering in a fire pot on flames, cooking on the back burner in the Master Chef's universal kitchen. It's been stewing for years, waiting to be served at the proper time, and it's fire-hot with brimstone. It's too hot to handle and will burn those spiritually poverty-stricken souls because the smoke coming from their torment will rise forever and ever (Revelation 14:11).

The candlelight shining from Jesus Christ will not be placed in the center of this table since those sitting at the table love darkness so much. Not even the master of darkness, Satan himself, who paraded around as an angel of light, can shine at this table due to the total darkness found in this dining room because *"complete darkness"* is held in reserve for this very special occasion.

In keeping with the Master Chef's excellent service He will serve this meal on His best china (a gold bowl and cup). He has given instructions to His head waiter to make sure all the courses were served by him and the six other skilled waiters experienced in serving this special variation of stew. These seven waiters *(the number seven means complete or perfect)* served the reserved table last. These waiters came out of the Master Chef's kitchen properly dressed for this occasion; clean and bright with gold aprons girded around their waist. You can see the smoke coming out of the kitchen as the waiters enter the dark dining room to serve the seven course stew, along with the cup of wine full of the King's fierce wrath. Once the stew is served; the Master Chef will utter similar words like those He said years ago, "It is done!" All the meals prepared by the Master Chef will be completed and finished to His satisfaction...Kitchen closed. (Revelation 15-17 – NASB)

"A Special Cup of Soup"

Prepared for Salvation

The Recipe for Salvation

A Special Cup of Soup Prepared for Salvation
The Recipe for Salvation

If you don't like dining in the dark on stew, then maybe you who have not accepted the King's invitation from the Master Chef to dine elsewhere will consider getting in the soup line to dine on a Cup of Soup prepared for salvation before it's too late to eat.

Your First Supper

This specially prepared soup is warm and inviting and easy enough to swallow for any poor and lost soul in need of the right Master to guide his or her life. There is nothing in this Cup of Soup for you not to "CHEW" on because it contains all of the blessings of God. It is soothing to the soul if you just accept what Christ has done for you and what He is offering you to become one of His children.

This portion of spiritual food, which is found in John 3:16, has been prepared for believers to share with all those who are not saved, because they are not safe without salvation. Nor do they have any access to the blessings of God's Word without first eating this Cup of Soup. You must be born again in order to enjoy the banquet meals that have been prepared for all of the King's kids. Don't allow any poor soul to be left with having to dine from the "Cup of Indignation," which the Master Chef prepared for all those who will continue to reject Him. This cup is filled with the wine of God's fury, which will cause those who drink it to reel and fall. It is full of God's undiluted rage and is a bitter cup full of wrath for the sinner to swallow. It contains the Master Chef's ingredients of torment and the full strength of burning sulfur prepared with fire-hot brimstone, too hot for anyone to handle. But Satan and all those who chose to follow him will have to deal with this terrible stew. (Revelation

14:10: "The same shall drink of the wine of the wrath of God, which is poured out without mixture into the cup of his indignation; and he shall be tormented with fire and brimstone in the presence of the holy angels, and in the presence of the Lamb.")

Sin has separated the sinner from God, the King, and the only way back to Him is to go through His Son, Jesus Christ. It is time for the unsaved to stop dining with Satan and dine with the King instead by feasting on the living Word. In order to dine sufficiently at the King's banqueting table (the Bible), they must first receive His invitation by accepting the Son of God, Jesus Christ, as their personal Lord and Savior.

God has a wonderful plan for every person's life. If they desire to experience the full and meaningful abundance of life, inheriting all the promises and blessings given to every child of God, then they must surrender their wills to the King and accept the fullness of His Son, Jesus Christ, because Salvation has not been put on a layaway plan. God allowed His Son to be laid away for three days and then rise again for us to receive the fullness of Christ when Jesus paid for our salvation in full. It was fully planned out from the foundation of the world. God offered His only begotten Son so that whosoever believes in Him will receive eternal life, because God so loved the world. They can do this by faith and repeat this simple prayer. (Romans 10:9-10)

Please spend a few moments to share this recipe for salvation with those outside the kingdom of God so that they too will be filled with the Aged Royal Wine and receive a blessing for eternity and inherit the promise of the King when they become a prince or princess in the royal kingdom of God.

THE SINNER'S PRAYER

Lord, I need You. Thank You for dying on the cross for my sins. Please forgive me. I open the door to my heart and receive You as my personal Lord and Savior. Thank You for forgiving me of my sins and giving me eternal life. Now, take control of my life and make me the kind of person You want me to be. In Jesus's name I pray. Amen.

Note: If you have prayed this prayer to be saved, you are now born again and considered by God to be one of His children. I encourage you, as a new believer in Christ, to continue praying and read the Bible every day. Then, find a Bible-teaching church that you can call "home."

If you have just led someone else to pray this prayer, encourage your new brother or sister to either come to church with you or join a Bible-teaching church, where he or she can be surrounded by newly adopted brothers and sisters in Christ and grow into a strong and healthy Christian. Remember, saints, these new believers will not be served another Cup of Soup, so don't let them get back in the soup line once they have accepted God's invitation to come into His house and dine at His *"BIG"* banquet table! He wants them to feast on His rich and wonderful spiritual meals. They won't have to get in line there, because there are no lines at the banquet table of God . . . just sit down and eat a *"big dinner."* (Luke 14:16-17"...a certain man was giving a big dinner, and he invited many; ...to those who had been invited, come; for everything is ready now." God wants everyone to be able to sit down at His dinner table to taste His delicious meals and drink His sweet wine.

If you happen to be reading this book and you made a decision to accept Christ as your Personal Master Chef (Lord and Savior, Jesus Christ), then ask Him to take you by the hand and "dance" with you. You need Him to guide and direct you to the place where He has ordained for you to go and begin your Christian journey as you continue to dine at His banquet table.

Don't worry because you will be waited on by a host of angels that have been assigned and instructed by the Master Chef to render their services to wait on you hand and foot to assist you in your salvation. Hebrews 1:14 "Are they not all ministering spirits, sent out to render services for the sake of those who will inherit salvation?" (NASB)

The King, the angels and all of His children rejoice and welcome our newly adopted brother or sister in Christ into the Holy Family of God. Please, take your seat at the banqueting table, and dine on the Word of God until your heart is content.

God Bless You, Sweet Prince or Princess!

Spiritual
Culinary Glossary

The Definition of Words & Terms
For
The Spiritual Culinary 5 Book Series

Spiritual Culinary Glossary

The vocabulary listed below consists of culinary terms used allegorically in all five Spiritual Recipe Books for Godly Living.

After-Dinner Mints – The promises we receive from the King and the Master Chef, Jesus Christ, to say "Thank You for Dining with Us."

Appetizers – *Words and terms* used in the Bible that stimulate the appetite.

Bitter Herbs – Bad characteristics that are disagreeable, distasteful, or distressing, leading to the pain and suffering of a prince or princess of the King.

Bon Appétit – A French term that means (I Wish You) a hearty appetite.

Bonjour – French term that means *Hello.*

Bowl of Stew for Damnation *(STEW - Souls Tasting Eternal Wrath)* – A special dish of leftovers prepare by the Master Chef which contains the anger and wrath of God for all those who chose to hate and reject His Son, Jesus Christ. This meal has all the ingredients from the bitter herbs and spices of wickedness, sin, evil, disobedience and rebellion; along with a cup of wine of His bitter fury added to enhance the flavor of God's hatred of sin and immorality.

BYOB – *"Bring Your Own Bible"* Good practice to carry your own bible so you can read from it at church and study from it at home.

Calorie Desserts – Characters that possess bad qualities or characteristics and produce sin in their life by being disobedient to the King.

CHEW – Christians Having Eternal Wealth.

Chewing – Taking the necessary time to meditate on the Word of God.

Compliments to the Master Chef – Praises and words of gratitude to express your appreciation of the meals and what you tasted and experienced from the Master Chef that was good for you and to you.

Cuisine – The manner of preparing spiritual food.

Cup of Soup for Salvation – The passage of Scripture (John 3:16) that gives the unsaved soul a message of salvation that was specially prepared by the Master Chef to warm the heart and invite the sinner to repent and accept Jesus Christ as their Lord and Savior.

Du Jour – French term that means *of or from the day.* it also means *special to that day.*

Decorum – Good behavior or taste in conduct that adheres to customs and polite manners with a godly fear of offending the King.

Desserts – A course of *characters* in the Bible, served at the close of a spiritual meal.

Dietary Fiber of Knowledge – The necessary nutritional information required for your complete spiritual growth.

Digesting – Gaining an understanding of the Word of God by thinking over and arranging systematically in the mind; to comprehend.

Dining/Eating – To feed on the Word of God through reading; to take or consume by studying the Word of God.

Entrées – The main courses of study, that is, *chapters* in the Bible.

Etiquette – Table manners that govern your conduct in observance to the King's rules when spiritually eating. This includes the appropriate use of spiritual silverware utensils.

Exercise Program/Exercising – Personal application and practices of the Word of God that involve love, faith, obedience, forgiveness, prayer, and using your spiritual gifts.

Fat-Free Desserts – Characters that possess good qualities and characteristics that contain no form of sin.

Fat/Trans Fat – The sin in one's life that causes spiritual heart disease or spiritual death.

Feast – An elaborate meal, or banquet, of spiritual food that gives an unusual abundance of pleasure.

Fine Dining – Reading and studying the Word of God to gain a higher level of spiritual maturity.

Flavors – A savory blend of predominant qualities in the characteristics of a believer that distinguishes him or her from those outside the family of God—that is, the "Fruit of the Spirit" listed in Galatians 5. The flavors consist of joy, peace, patience, kindness, goodness, faithfulness, gentleness, and self-control.

Free Radicals of Temptation – The sinful schemes Satan uses to attack the weak parts of the spiritual body's immune system. They are unstable and highly reactive and can damage the spiritual body because they accelerate the progression of spiritual cancer and cardiovascular diseases that affect the heart.

Generation to Generation – The way in which biblical instructions were passed down from Genesis to Revelation.

Great Recipe Book – The sacred Scriptures of the Bible, comprised of Old and New Testaments.

"God, You & I" Dance ("G" "U" and "I" Dance) – Guidance; to perform rhythmic guiding movements provided by God, who leads and directs us His way in order to properly direct you through this life. (Very Special Treat: "Steppin' In The Name of The Lord.")

Healthy Dietary Program – A compilation of the impressive good qualities and characteristics of those in the Bible; a list of those life-changing behaviors, attitudes, habits, personalities, characteristics, and practices that will enhance your life if emulated.

House Salad – Main verse used to summarize the meaning of the chapter.

Ingredients – The main theme or themes of a chapter.

Just Say "NO NO" – The "No Bible, No Breakfast" rule that should be practiced everyday to ensure we feed our spiritual bodies before we feed our physical bodies.

Marinate – To soak in what you have learned to enrich the flavor of the Word.

Master Chef – Jesus Christ, who is the Head, who holds the authority and skills to teach and spiritually guide, and who directed those used to assist in preparing the sixty-six meals of the Bible.

Master Meal Plan – Jesus's plan for us to spend eternity with Him.

Meals – The sixty-six books of the Bible.

Menu – A overview of what today's Christian can expect to find dealing with certain issues in a particular book selected to read and study.

Menu Lessons – A list of questions served after a spiritual meal to gain spiritual knowledge and maturity.

Mise en Place – The process used to arrange or prepare for studying the Word of God.

Pack a Lunch – A place (Index Box) where your recorded "memory verses" of Scripture on index cards are stored to refer to while dining on you physical lunch.

Personally Prescribed Spiritual Vitamins & Supplements – The essential substances of *praise* and *worship* that provide energy for building up your spiritual immune system.

Prince – A male member of the royal family of God and a son of the King, noble in rank and status.

Princess – A female member of the royal family of God and a daughter of the King, outstanding and possessing the beautiful, quiet spirit that the King honors.

Recipe of Meals – A summary of the books in the Bible.

Royal Attire – The Full Armor of God, a garment of spiritually fine white linen made of faith and love, to be worn by a prince and princess as they go about their day to protect them against evil and the Evil One. The six-piece attire is:

1. ***Belt of Truth*** – To practice a life of honesty and truthfulness.

2. ***Breastplate of Righteousness*** – The righteous character and deeds of the believer, which are full of faith and love.
3. ***Feet Shod*** – The preparation of the gospel of peace, which is the firm foundation, which we are to stand on to spread the gospel.
4. ***Shield of Faith*** – God's protection against all the attacks of our spiritual enemy, Satan.
5. ***Helmet of Salvation*** – A crown of wisdom and discernment that represents the mind of Christ and carries an engraving that says "Holiness to the Lord."
6. ***Sword of the Spirit*** – The Word of God, the offensive weapon used to combat all of Satan's lies.

Royal Candlelight – Jesus Christ is the special Light centered on the King's banquet table, considered while dining on a spiritual meal.

Royal Candlelight Devotional Moments – Sitting daily before the presence of the King to read one or two chapters of the Bible, preferably in the mornings before you start your busy day.

Royal Court – The church and the kingdom of God.

Royalty – The special characteristics of the prince and princess that are peculiar but acceptable in conduct, speech, and appearance in representing the King. They are of superior status, power, and position and have a privileged class of kingly ancestry with high ranks and high standing.

Salads – Individual *verses* in the Bible.

Seasoning – To converse with or address God in prayer to enhance the natural flavors of His Word and make it palatable to us in order to taste and see that the Lord is good.

Side Dishes – Instructions to help remind you of what is necessary to fully enjoy the meal before you start to dine.

Soul-Food Menus – Instructions prepared from the heart of the Master Chef, Jesus Christ, in which God expresses His love for us.

Sous Chefs – The apostles, prophets, evangelists, pastors, and teachers: the authors, with various cultural backgrounds, of the sixty-six books of the Bible.

Special Treats – The unique way of studying God's Word that will bring unexpected joy and delight to the soul.

Spices – The love that God uses in His Word, giving zest to all its spiritual ingredients.

Spiritual A La Carte – The Spiritual Gourmet Chef's Spiritual Menu of actual individual dishes prepared for your physical dining pleasure that is listed separately from God's Menu and dishes.

Spiritual Connoisseurs – Spiritual culinary professionals who are not ashamed of the gospel, but use their spiritual gifts to spread the gospel and build up the body of Christ.

Spiritual Culinary Skills – Spiritual gifts that are given to you by the Holy Spirit.

Spiritual Dinner Table – The special place where you choose to study the Word of God.

Spiritual Food – Truths, teachings, and principles relating to sacred matters that nourish, sustain, guide, and supply the spiritual body.

Spiritual Food-Borne Illnesses – The spiritual viruses, parasites, and bacteria that Satan has control over and uses to contaminate and attack every believer of God's Word (Ephesians 6:12).

Spiritual Maturity – The personal, spiritual characteristics of a mature Christian due to his or her continued spiritual growth by studying and applying the Word of God.

Spiritual Proteins – The natural components found in the Word of God that God provides for His children to guarantee their holiness and righteousness in Him.

Spiritual Utensils – The resource tools used to successfully study the Word of God. The five-piece spiritual flatware is:
     Sharp Knife – Study Bible
     Dinner Fork – Concordance
     Salad Forks – Bible Dictionary and Bible Encyclopedia
     Dinner Spoon – Commentary
     Dessert Fork – Handbook

Spiritual Breakfast Bar or Snack – Reading one or two chapters in the Bible every morning.

Spiritual Vegetables and Fruits – Verses of Scripture that include parables, miracles, prayers, events, and the Lord's conversations with people.

STEW – Souls Tasting Eternal Wrath. A meal prepared for Damnation.

Stock – The foundation used to create the base in each meal.

Swallowing – Understanding God's Word by absorbing what you have meditated upon and accepting the word of truth without question, protest, or resentment.

Sweet Herbs – The compassion that God uses to bring out the genuine qualities expressed in His Word.

Sweet Treats – The blessings we receive from the King and the Master Chef, Jesus Christ, to say "Thank You for Dining with Us."

Table Manners – The proper way in which we are to dine at the King's table.

Taste – Various levels of understanding.

The King – God, who is the Ruler of life and of His heavenly kingdom.

The Lamb – Jesus Christ, the special main ingredient used as the foundational stock in every meal, showing the tender, sweet, dear, and gentle sacrificial parts of our Lord and Savior.

The Aged Royal Wine – The Holy Spirit, who is the active presence of God in human life, constituting the Third Person of the Trinity. We should spiritually drink of the Holy Spirit every day for spiritual guidance and direction to assist us in our obedience toward the King.

The Royal Family Secret Ingredient – The various characteristics of Jesus Christ demonstrated in each book of the Bible.

Weight-Loss Program – Life-changing application based on our own list of sins committed by the characters in the Bible, as well as our own personal sins that we have learned of that offend the King and need to be eliminated from our spiritual bodies.

Vol-Au-Dent of Fruit – Spiritual puff pastry filled with specially prepared characters, who were perfectly fruitful in their obedience to God.

Yeast – Self-rising traces of pride or arrogance, causing haughty behaviors that make the believer appear "puffed up" in his or her attitude, which is displeasing and destructive because of selfish motives and attitudes toward God and others.

Note: Yeast or leaven is a Biblical symbol of sin.

Your Spiritual Gourmet Chef's Culinary Artistry

Lynn Williams is a Certified Gourmet Chef with a Culinary Arts Degree in French cooking, receiving her college degree in culinary arts and hotel management. Her education extends to art, floral designing, interior designing, and decoration. She is the founder of The Royal Candlelight Christian Publishing Company. She has established her career as an author, workshop presenter, Bible study teacher at The Teleois Institute and Ministry Director for Vacation Bible School, events planning, special projects and the political awareness ministries at Ecclesia Christian Fellowship, located in San Bernardino, California, one of California's well-known churches in the community and in the Inland Empire.

Lynn has owned her catering, floral designing, wedding, and events-planning business for over twenty-five years. She has also developed her own line of Christian books called The Royal Candlelight Christian Book Series. This series is being developed to point you to the truth, which can only be found in the Word of God. Five of the books will be "spiritual recipe books" written in culinary allegory, aiding study of all sixty-six books of the Bible. Other titles released will be based on life experiences and various life situations written in allegory to encourage the true believer of God by assisting them in finding the truth about what God has to say about their life challenges according to the governing principles of His Word.

Lynn is dedicated to humbly serving God and His people by taking every opportunity to minister, love, give, and cater to "picking up the broken pieces in the lives of believers."

CONTACT US:

We want to hear from you about this book. Also, if you are interested in Lynn's line of Christian books and want us to contact you on all new releases and author interviews, please log on to:

www.royalcandlelight.com
info@royalcandlelight.com
Internet TV Website: Ustream tv.com (Royal Candlelight)

72483898R00123

Made in the USA
Columbia, SC
20 June 2017